AF348539

From
Hitler
to
Pearl Harbor

Untold Stories:
One Man's Navy Adventures

Volume I:
The War Before the War, 1940-1941

Richard E. Cragg
Lieutenant Commander USNR Retired

ISBN 0-7414-1644-1

Published by:

INFI∞ITY
PUBLISHING.COM

519 West Lancaster Avenue
Haverford, PA 19041-1413
Info@buybooksontheweb.com
www.buybooksontheweb.com
Toll-free (877) BUY BOOK
Local Phone (610) 520-2500
Fax (610) 519-0261

Printed in the United States of America

Printed on Recycled Paper

Published December 2003

Contents

Dedications

Joan Odine Yeager (JOY) Cragg – unexpectedly deceased, December 29, 2000 – my greatly missed wife, partner, and schoolmate. I reluctantly returned to school again just to be with her.

Dr. Robin Cragg Barr, PhD, Linguist-in-Residence at American University, tireless researcher, critic, and daughter. She is friendly too.

Philip George Cragg, BSEE, son and Professional Engineer who keeps straightening out the horrible messes my computer gets into.

Lawrence Richard Cragg, son and Professional Musician who, with his siblings, has been pressing me for years to write down the yarns they have heard all their lives.

Father Leon Mertensotto, STD, CSC, of Notre Dame, tireless researcher, critic, and friend.

Professor Blake Wiley, MA, of Manatee Community College, Mentor, critic, editor, and friend, who encouraged me to keep going after the death of Joan when I was going to quit.

Art Hoffman of Harbert, Michigan, who has sent me

important articles and has always been encouraging and enthusiastic.

Dorothy Shawhan Cragg, MA – deceased November 21, 1977 – who shared my adventures in the sequel to this book – now in the process of being written. This sequel will include my solution to a German U-boat *Enigma* cipher machine problem while I was officer in charge of Research and Development at the Naval Code and Signal Laboratory.

Manatee Community College of Florida, which provided the academic atmosphere needed to provoke my writing.

All those on my mailing list who faithfully read my writing and, hopefully, enjoyed it.

Author's Preface

The title of this book and the other volumes in this series is a little misleading. By *Untold Stories*, I mean those parts of my varied experiences in the Navy before and during World War II which are not generally known. Some of these adventures are unusual, or from an unusual perspective; some have been kept secret for many years; and some, though not technically secret, still are hard to believe. I include in this volume some tales of shipboard life from the perspective of an engineer in the 'black gang' of the engine room, stories of my voyages ranging across half the globe from New Zealand to Iceland, and details of the Navy's actions (often hidden) to defend the United States against Japan and Germany even before the official start of World War II. In the next volume, I describe my then-secret experiences in the Naval Code and Signal Lab during World War II, working on our cipher machines and also helping solve the German U-boat *Enigma* cipher machine problem for the United States Navy.

But in a different sense, many of these tales could instead be termed 'Oft-told Stories'. Some of these adventures are familiar to my family and friends, from years of hearing me relate anecdotes about the South Pacific and unlikely facts about our apparent 'piracy' in the North Atlantic before the start of the war. My family, especially, pressed me to make a record of these events so that this obscure but important part of our history would not be lost, but for a long time I hesitated, thinking that this task might better be left to others who had more facility with the typewriter keyboard, or easier access to accurate historical records.

Not until I was in my eighties did I begin to think that if I didn't tell these stories, then they might never be told. I was reluctantly persuaded to return to school at Manatee Community College in Florida, though I already had my bachelor's degree. My dear wife Joan convinced me to accompany her so she would have a schoolmate, and then I was encouraged by the English courses we took to think that I might have a shot at finally getting my adventures down on paper after all. My children provided me with a computer and with much coaching, I went to work. In the *Dedications* section above, I thank those who helped and inspired me in this endeavor.

The names, dates, and places in these stories are as accurate as I can make them after the passage of sixty years and more. I apologize if some names or dates are omitted or even faulty, because I couldn't dredge them up, but the experiences are all true, as I lived them.

Several of these chapters have been published in the magazine of the *U.S. Navy Cruiser Sailors Association*. I sincerely thank Editor Mr. Edward J. August for his kindness in accepting and printing this author's chronicles in such a well printed and put-together publication.

1
Wolf Packs

U-boat wolf packs? Why are they called wolf packs? This is a misnomer. Submarines are not wolves; they are lethal sharks – clustering in, perhaps, schools? They are out there waiting for us – oh, yes, we know they are there. And they know we are coming. As we near each underwater ambush laid for us, German radio messages increase to a telltale flood. Though we can't read them because of their incredibly complex ciphering known as *Enigma*, the mere quantity of messages is enough to tell us the U-boats are being informed of our approach. But we must risk our passage through trap after trap, cost what it may.

There is yet another ugly omen stressing our peril. These 'sharks', Hitler's pets, had been in a 'feeding frenzy', as sharks will, only a day before our tempting U.S. Navy Task Force came into their ken. We have been steaming through an ocean strewn with sickening evidence of this frenzy. Wreckage and – yes, bodies too – are pushed aside by our bows as they slice the seas over the Grand Banks of the North Atlantic. This pitiful flotsam can be seen only as it emerges out of the dense fog so characteristic of the Banks. Our Task Force is close behind a large British convoy from Halifax, Nova Scotia – desperately trying to bring its vital cargo to Murmansk on the Arctic shore of Russia. Hitler's U-boats have exacted a terrible toll from this ill-fated convoy, and remain lurking, lying in wait for us to come near.

Could there be a bright spot in this awful carnage? Yes! Unbelievably, one of the destroyers has come upon a lifeboat with seven Red Cross nurses and some seamen – still alive after the terrifying ordeal of the torpedoing and sinking of their ship. The fog is so thick that the unseen battleship **U.S.S. New York** ahead of us is towing a splashing 'chip'(float) for us to always keep in view from the wing of the bridge. As long as we keep it alongside of us, we will stay in line with the **New York,** and won't run into her. Even our own bow is invisible from the bridge. (There is yet no Radar for us.) The destroyer came close enough in this fog to spot the lifeboat and yet did not run it down. Incredible luck! In these cold waters and chilly air, all would have perished of hypothermia had they not been rescued in time. We jokingly wish the nurses would be transferred to our ship, the light cruiser **U.S.S. Brooklyn**, for we have lots more room – and our medical staff is headed by Dr. Manlove – a Commander, not a Lieutenant (jg).

As each ambuscade of U-boats is sensed by the destroyer 'Sonars', the 'general quarters' alarm is sounded in all ships – and woe betide any hand who does not report to his battle station within five minutes, for in five minutes the water tight doors and hatches in all ships are 'dogged down'- not to be opened until permission of the Captain is granted. Now, if struck by a torpedo, we won't sink as fast for there are many sealed compartments for flotation. It is told that the British battle cruiser **H.M.S. Hood** sank within minutes after one hit from the **Bismarck** because it did not have many small compartments, but only very large ones.

As we wait at our posts, the 'whumps' of exploding depth charges can be felt on our hull as the destroyers rush about their duty of protecting five precious transport ships from the ravaging submarines. I, as an officer in my battle station in the after engine room, am below the waterline where the thuds are felt most strongly. After emerging from battle stations, we are told that a German U-boat has been sunk! Fittingly, this is the Fourth of July complete with fireworks. On arrival at our destination, Iceland, the final count is disclosed – two submarines sunk, and a probable third!

Two questions – though not at war with Germany in July, 1941, we are sinking its ships! How could this be? My first thought is that sinking ships of another country could be termed 'piracy' if we are not at war, though we are all angry with Germany after seeing what we have been seeing. Also, what am I doing as an officer in the Navy in a powerful combat ship – when a little over a year ago, I was an enlisted man in Chicago – a Fireman 3rd Class? The following chapters will answer these questions and describe my adventures in the Navy during the year and a half before the war officially began for the United States on December 7, 1941.

2
Early Days

I am a native Chicagoan, growing up on the South Side of Chicago, two and a half miles north of the University of Chicago. I was thoroughly familiar with the University's gray limestone Gothic architecture since I went to the University of Chicago Lab Schools, including the high school. I walked to school every day from the fourth grade on (five miles round trip), picking up my best friend Dick Schwartz[1] a mile into the trip.

My two older brothers also attended these schools, as did my cousin Elwood Atherton, who lived with us. Elwood and my brother Hank also went on to attend the University of Chicago, but I was contrary and went to Purdue, instead, since their engineering program was outstanding and the University of Chicago had no engineering program at all. I could save Depression money[2] too by living on my brother Tom's farm

---

[1] For some unlikely coincidences and narrow escapes involving Dick Schwartz, my neighbor Salmon O. Levinson, and the notorious Leopold and Loeb, see Appendix 2: *Salmon O. Levinson.*

[2] My father had died when I was only thirteen, and money was tight.

4

two and a half miles away from the Purdue campus.

During my freshman year at Purdue, I rode a bicycle back and forth to campus, where I parked it at my fraternity, Phi Kappa Sigma. In my sophomore year, I scraped up enough money to buy an ancient (1927) F-head Harley-Davidson motorcycle (later to be traded in on a 1937 Harley 74 cu.in.).

Purdue, being a 'land grant' college, had compulsory ROTC training. The training was exclusively Field Artillery - practicing with French '75' field guns and much complicated foot drill. There was no rifle drill at all. The foot drill came in handy years later when I was in the Naval Reserve. I made Sergeant by the end of my Sophomore year when the compulsory part was complete.

I received my BSEE (Bachelor of Science in Electrical Engineering) from Purdue in 1938, having just turned 21 the month before, and went to work for the Duncan Electric Company in Lafayette, Indiana. A year later, my then-fiancee Barbara Washburn (who appears tangentially in the following tales) came to Chicago from Oregon to live with her aunt, so I got a job at the Commonwealth Edison Company in Chicago to be closer to her.

My experiences at the Lab Schools were pivotal in my later decisions for two reasons: the shop class gave me a background in mechanics and first led me to think that I might be able to invent things[3]; and my experiences with bullies made me hate any kind of bullying, including Hitler's actions, and also helped me feel I could do something about it. I had been the victim of bullying since kindergarten, since I grew faster than my muscles could keep up with. I was tall, but clumsy and weak until puberty. After the hormones kicked in, I didn't realize at first that I had become strong.

---

[3] I have now been granted a number of patents, but my Navy inventions couldn't be patented because of their secret nature.

But one day when I was fourteen, as I was being chased around the locker room preparatory to my customary beating, I pivoted and landed a right to the jaw of my pursuer. To my astonishment, and that of the onlookers, he collapsed to the floor and remained unconscious for a full minute. I thought I had killed him. He came to, held his jaw, groaned, and made no effort to go after me as I had feared. In fact, he avoided me, as did the other bullies, after a few of them tried me out, only to get licked. The school guard, Mr. Ford, saw the whole affair. I thought surely he would haul me into the Principal's office. He didn't do anything. I have since thought Mr. Ford had seen me bullied many times, and felt my 'victim' had it coming. Thank you Mr. Ford.

This one punch and its results gave me enough self-confidence to believe that bullies could be defeated if one stood up to them, and led me eventually to enlist in the Naval Reserve, as described in the next chapter. I consider Adolf Hitler to be the foulest bully of our time, and I was in a position where I could actively support my country against him.

My machine shop teacher Eugene C. Wittick, a graduate engineer, became a father figure to me in my senior year of high school. Under his guidance, I became familiar with all manner of the sophisticated machines in the shop. I could operate them all, from drill press to milling machine.[4] I had never realized that I had any aptitude for mechanical things, but I learned from Mr Wittick how things are made, which was important in my later career as an inventor. Some of us used to congregate at his house in the evenings, where he had a pistol range set up in his basement and we practiced 'plinking' with his .22 automatic. He had been a Radioman in the World War I Navy, and described his experiences in the Illinois Naval

---

[4]I wasn't allowed to use the big planer, since it was monopolized by some guy from the University of Chicago who was making apparatus for measuring the speed of light.

Militia (later U.S. Naval Reserve), among which was the shelling and sinking of a captured German submarine whose wreck is now lying on the bed of Lake Michigan off of Chicago. He had a lot to do with my joining the Naval Reserve.

Another important part of my background is the many hours I spent on the water. My family spent summers in Lakeside, Michigan, on the shores of Lake Michigan (as can be guessed by the name), and I would take every opportunity I could to sail. My familiarity with boats and water inclined me towards the Navy, rather than another branch of the armed services, and my experience stood me in good stead later in the sailing whaleboat races in Hawaii (described in Chapter 15, *Under Sail in Pearl Harbor*).

3
Enlisting

"Why do you want to join the Naval Reserve?" asked Commander Brown. This was my moment of truth. The Commander, an officer in the Regular Navy attached to the Chicago Naval Reserve, was the one whose endorsement, sent to Washington, spelled "Yes" or "No" to my application for a commission.

My mother, Miriam Thomas Cragg, wise and intensely patriotic, despised Hitler and his Nazis. It is argued by some revisionists today, trying to excuse America's apathy, that Americans had not been told about the death camps in Germany, but the newspapers certainly did tell us! We *were* told! I remember reading about those camps in the papers. Though we are not Jewish, Mother was just as horrified as if we were. She thought Hitler was dangerous, and we would be at war before long. Mother's friends asked, "Why do you get so upset about that stupid little man with his silly Charlie Chaplin mustache?" Mother talked a lot with me – and I had read *The Road to War* by historian Walter Millis about World War I. That book convinced me that our entry into war with Germany was inevitable. Mother was also fearful of Japan – she belonged to an organization titled "Stop Arming Japan". This group endeavored to prevent selling scrap iron and steel to Japan. When successful, the group made the papers. Its motto was: "Iron and steel supplied to Japan will be returned to us with deadly force!" How true!

The result of Mother's confiding in me, and of my own reasoning, was that in the spring of 1940 I went to the Naval Reserve Armory at the foot of Randolph Street for the purpose of enlisting. As I filled out the enlistment forms, the Chief Petty Officer, looking over my shoulder, said, excitedly, "You're a college graduate and an engineer? You could get a probationary commission as an engineering duty only (EDO) Ensign. After a two-year correspondence course with the book of Navy Regulations as your textbook, your commission would be permanent." "That sounds good," I said. "Let me apply for that – but in the meantime, I still want to enlist, just in case the commission doesn't come through." And that's the way we did it. The Chief told me about my coming interview with Commander Brown. He cautioned, "Good luck. He's tough!"

How was I going to handle the Commander's question about why I wanted to enlist? If I was honest, my cause could be lost if his name were spelled B-r-a-u-n, as in Eva Braun, Hitler's mistress, instead of B-r-o-w-n, and he was involved with the nest ('bund') of Nazis – publicly active in the Chicago area (even parading). I was honest and told him I found Hitler and his cohorts to be loathsome. I thought we would soon be at war because of Hitler, and, in my judgment, being somewhat skilled in sailing and around water, I would be of more use to the Navy than to the Army. "Are you Jewish?" "No, Commander," I replied, "but I still hate what Hitler is doing." I told him a bit about Mother. He said, "I admire your mother, and thoroughly agree with her – and with you. I am going to endorse your application favorably. Good luck!"

Going back to the Chief, I told him what the Commander had said. The Chief said, "Great! Good for you!

It isn't going to do *me* any harm for finding you and steering you to him. Now let's get you a uniform." I went home equipped with my new outfit, and with instructions to go to the Naval Reserve Armory every Tuesday night, reporting to Division 22. Mother wanted to see me in the uniform, and said she was proud.

The next Tuesday, three Divisions of twenty men each met in the Armory drill hall to be formed for review. The drill was easy for me except for the rifle drill. Purdue ROTC was for Field Artillery training with no rifle drill at all, but the Navy foot drill was simple compared to Purdue, so there were no 'goof-ups' on my part. I wished later that I had memorized the rifle drill while performing it. There are some orders which, if given in the wrong order, result in chaos. For example 'About Face' following right after 'Present Arms' is an impossible and idiotic sequence (but fun to watch).

The Naval Reserve had some 'pulling boats' – heavy launches which had to be rowed. Volunteers were asked to try out for Saturday rowing competitions between the Divisions. I volunteered. In spite of my noble efforts, Division 22 didn't do well. An officer was in charge of each boat, and did the steering. On one occasion, when we were coming into the dock for a landing, Lieutenant (jg) Neal was steering. Mr. Neal should have told us to stop rowing and 'toss oars' sooner, and we were going too fast to stop. We over-shot the dock and rammed into a motor yacht passing by. An angry woman put out her head and yelled, "You bunch of Sea Scouts!" Years later, in 1949, my little girl, Laura, made a friend, Nancy Neal, who lived across the corner from us. After some polite and private conversation with him, it turned out that Nancy's Daddy was *that* Mr. Neal. He didn't seem to remember the incident. I would have forgotten it myself except I wasn't to blame – and it was funny.

We had instruction by the Petty Officers on Naval matters. I was taught to roll up my blues inside-out to get the proper inverted creases on the sides and in-seams of the pants. I still know how to tie the kerchief so the ends are square, not vertical. I also know the thirteen buttons on that front flap stood for the thirteen states. The three stripes on the dress blue collar were for Nelson's three victories in the Napoleonic War. (How about that – and who cares?) We were getting ready for our yearly adventure – two weeks afloat in a gunboat for our annual training cruise on Lake Michigan. We looked forward to the cruise. After all, *that* is what it was all about!

Figure 1, Fireman 3rd Class R.E.Cragg

4
U.S.S. Wilmington

She was a grand old lady, my first ship. Though the **U.S.S Wilmington** was only a gunboat, she had the look of a battleship, with armored conning tower topped with a 'fighting top' (armored crow's nest). Commissioned in 1893, she fought the Spanish in the battle of Santiago, Cuba, (1898) under Admiral Schley. Later, she was placed on the Yangtze River patrol. For that duty her round bottom was replaced with a 'skip-jack' (vee) bottom to reduce her draft for negotiating the notorious Yangtze rapids. In the China Sea during a typhoon, she endured the greatest list any U.S. Navy ship ever suffered without going over.[5]

Returning to America from China, and unaccompanied by a collier for refueling, **Wilmington** lacked the coal capacity to cross the Pacific. Sails were rigged on the conning tower and on a 'jury-rigged' mizzen mast, and she mostly sailed across.[6] After conversion to oil,

---

[5] I took this tale with a grain of salt, only to learn later from two separate and surprising sources that it was true. (See Chapter 6 for one of them.) The unlikelihood of surviving a 90 degree list had warranted our disbelief.

[6] I had read this story earlier in the United States Naval Institute Proceedings magazine. My cousin, Elwood Atherton, a 'Navy buff', had given me a membership to the Institute. My joining the Naval Reserve was strongly influenced by this.

using 'Mayflower'[7] burners, she became one of five gunboats on the Great Lakes (one for each Lake), and was based in Cleveland, Ohio, on Lake Erie. These gunboats were used for annual Naval Reserve training cruises on Lake Michigan. A Regular Navy crew was attached to each ship to augment the Reserve crew.

Wilmington carried two 5-inch guns,[8] and target practice and maneuvers were performed daily during a cruise. Each ship took its turn in towing the target raft, a risky job. The towing ship sometimes was hit instead of the target, according to tales told us by the Regular crewmen. Every evening, the ships anchored in the bay formed by the crescent moon of South Manitou Island. A snug anchorage – it was protected from unlikely easterly storms by the bulk of the Michigan mainland, and from all other directions by the horns of South Manitou Island's crescent. The middle weekend in Traverse City, Michigan, 67 miles distant, and located on Grand Traverse Bay, was fun except for those on watch who must stay aboard to keep the ship's machinery going. I missed Sunday liberty because of standing fire room watch.

Wilmington was a primitive ship in many respects, but changes are not necessarily improvements. Instead of modern berths which uncomfortably reflect every roll of the ship, we slept in old-fashioned hammocks suspended six feet above the deck. As the ship rolled, it rotated about us as we remained stationary in our hammocks, oblivious to the rough

---

[7] Named for the presidential yacht **Mayflower**, which was changed from coal burning to oil burning using the burners invented (it is said) for the **Mayflower**. These self contained burners do not require a pressurized fire room to provide 'forced draft' (as do ships originally built as oil burners).

[8] By treaty with Canada, which feared invasion from our Gunboats (kidding my Canadian born Mentor, Blake Wiley), no United States ship on the Great Lakes is allowed to have more than two major guns, not to exceed five inches in caliber.

seas. Each morning the hammocks were taken down and rolled in neat 'sausages,' each lashed with a single line, tied in the prescribed thirteen hitches representing the thirteen original states. The hammocks were then stowed in bins just inside the armor plating of the ship. In time of combat, these solidly rolled hammocks served to lessen danger to the crew by absorbing flying fragments if the ship was hit.

What was really primitive was the crew's toilet or 'head'.[9] The crew's toilet was a fore and aft 'head rail', situated over a long inclined trough with running water. Sitting on this plank, and hanging over the running water, was how the crew used the head. An occasion to remember was when someone, probably one of the Regulars, floated a burning wad of paper at the high end of the trough. The result was great sport. I saw 'Jumping-Jacks' as the flame passed under each butt down the line.

Reporting for duty in July of 1940, Fireman 3rd Class R. E. Cragg went up the 'brow' (gangplank) shouldering his sea-bag. Not quite the same was the experience of a wealthy high-schoolmate of mine, Herman Ritzwoller, whose *chauffeur*, after much arguing, was not allowed to carry Herman's sea-bag on board for him. As a Seaman 2nd Class, Herman out-ranked me (there is nothing lower than a Fireman 3rd Class[10]), but I didn't envy him one bit. With a start like that, Herman was given the worst jobs in the ship. I saw him with his white uniform drenched with blood from the meat cutting he did as a 'galley slave'. But 'Ritzy' ended the cruise as one of the most popular members of the crew. He did everything asked, with a willing smile. Herman is now listed in the directory of the Retired Officers Association. In World War II, Herman earned his

---

[9]To find out how the 'HEAD' got its name, see Appendix 3: *Head Rails and Poop Decks.*

[10]For a list of Navy ranks and ratings, see Appendix 1: *A Primer for Landlubbers.*

commission as a Chief Warrant Officer. Good for him! That took a lot of 'doing'.

Rumor had it that I might get a commission. Because of this, and because I was an engineer, I was given the position (way above my rating) as throttle-man on the port (or 'junior') engine. A Machinist's Mate, 1st Class ran the starboard engine. It was great fun to operate what I had only heard about, an antique 'triple expansion' steam engine with its three cylinders which got progressively bigger as the steam expanded from one to the other. To balance this favoritism, I also had the task of compartment cleaner. It was my duty to keep the compartment in which I lived ready for inspection at any time. This meant sweeping and swabbing the deck. Also, I disposed of any trash which might find its way into my domain.

We had some good times, such as a 'sing-along' presided over by the Regulars. I remember one of the sea chanteys, at least one verse and the chorus:

Oh the Manitou fisher-women haven't any combs.
Look-away, look-away.
They comb their hair with codfish bones.
We're bound for Australia.

Chorus:
Look-away my bully, bully boys.
Look-away, look-away.
Look-away, and don't you make a noise.
We're bound for Australia.

There was also a cookout on the Manitou Island beach. A fellow fraternity brother of mine from Purdue, Charles Musson, was also a fellow enlisted man in my Division. We decided to explore South Manitou Island and we got lost. By the time we got back to the beach, it was dark, and the last shore boat had left! Fortunately, there were quite a few others who had also missed the boat. After we signaled by waving burning branches, a boat came back for us. Immediately on return to the ship we were all 'put on report.' The next day, we were lined up and chewed out by one of our Reserve officers, a full Lieutenant, Mr. Severin. I thought, "There goes my chance for a commission."

Not so! On my return home, my commission was waiting for me in the mail! That was the end of my 'distinguished' enlisted career, complete with being put on report. Now I am an Ensign!

PS: My first Navy paycheck for 15 days of active duty was $10.16. Firemen 3rd Class were paid $21.00 per month (still on World War I pay scale), but the Commonwealth Edison Company of Chicago patriotically gave me these two weeks off with full pay in addition to my regular paid vacation. (The Chief Electrical Engineer of the Edison Company, William F. 'Bill' Sims, was one of the organizers of the Illinois Naval Militia after World War I, and had a lot to do with this. While on active duty during World War II, my Edison Company raises and promotions continued as if I was there!)

Figure 2. **U.S.S. Wilmington** PG-8   USN Archives
This picture was taken when **Wilmington** was a coal burner.
The stack is quite tall and slender compared to the shorter and
'fatter' stack after conversion to an oil burner. Wilmington was
white as befitting a part of Teddy Roosevelt's 'Great White
Fleet". She was painted grey 'war color' and was an oil burner
when I was in her.

5
Sink or Swim

"I thought I would throw him in to see if he would sink or swim," Admiral Evers, Commandant of the Ninth District Naval Reserve, was heard to say to his guests Tuesday night at the Naval Reserve Armory. I found out later what he had said. It's just as well I didn't hear him; I was nervous enough as it was.

A big ceremony had been made of Fireman 3rd Class Cragg's promotion to Ensign. Still in enlisted uniform and in the ranks I heard the Officer of the Day (who represented the Captain) roar out, "Fireman Cragg, front and center!" Stepping out of the ranks, I made a sharp left turn, marched to the center, turned right, and saluted. After returning my salute, the Officer of the Day loudly read out my commission as Ensign. After another exchange of salutes, I 'About Faced' and marched back into ranks. There was applause from the guests gathered near the big doors. It felt good!

A week before, upon returning from our cruise, I had found my commission waiting in my mail. Going to a uniform company, *Bailey's*, where my friend Dick Schwartz's father, Judge U.S. Schwartz, had his riding clothes made, I was measured for my uniform. It was promised within two weeks. For fifty dollars, I bought the required sword. Using the Navy manual at home, I practiced the simple maneuvers required of a sword bearer: 'Present Arms,' 'Order Arms,' 'Salute' – I knew them all. I felt I was well prepared to participate in the Tuesday night review. The uniform was made in time, and I confidently went to the Armory for my first public appearance as an officer.

"Mr. Cragg, you are the Officer of the Deck tonight." "Oh, my Gosh," I thought, "I don't know how to form up the Divisions. I don't know the commands for rifle drill. I'm really in a mess." Let me explain my position: the Officer of the Day was in command. My job as Officer of the Deck was to form the three Divisions into ranks, and present them to the Officer of the Day. Oh, what a predicament! I knew how to *follow* the orders, but I didn't know how to *give* them. At least I knew what to do with my sword (except to stab myself, a tempting but impractical solution to my problem). Guests of the Admiral and of other officers were swarming around the entrance, perhaps some of the same people who had witnessed my promotion to Ensign, and would see what a fool I could make of myself. I did some fast thinking.

I made two assumptions: one, that the Officer of the Day was a good guy, and two, that he would realize that a bum show on my part would reflect badly on him. Marching out, I stood close to him, saluted him with my sword, and whispered, "What do I do?" Returning the salute, he whispered instructions. Making a snappy 'About Face', familiar to me from ROTC, I bellowed my commands. After another About Face and Salute, the next question was whispered, "What do I do now?" A good formula, it was repeated until we were through. There were never so many 'About Faces' and 'Salutes' performed at the review before. Some probably wondered. The result was a perfect presentation of the three Divisions to the Officer of the Day. I think we both came out of this situation very well, but I can still feel those grinding emotions.

President Roosevelt declared the country to be in a state of 'Limited National Emergency'; and inactive Naval Academy-trained Reserve officers began to appear at the Armory. During the Depression, those lucky enough to get into the Naval Academy, with its free education, found the upper half (academically) of each class placed on active duty in the Navy when graduated. The other half of the class was absorbed into civilian life, but remained in the inactive Reserves, subject to call to active duty in a National Emergency. These graduates had a good education to help them live as civilians. With things warming up in the world, many Reservists thought they had better practice being officers again, in case they were called back. When the first such Reserve Ensign appeared, he, too, was made Officer of the Deck on his first day back in uniform, but he had forgotten much since the Naval Academy. His solution was to get drunk. It was hilarious! There was never so much aimless waving about of a sword outside of a performance by a ham actor in a swashbuckler movie. The Officer of the Day could have been slain during this one sided 'duel'. After that, Admiral Evers stopped using the 'sink or swim' trick which had worked so well on me. The Naval Academy graduate was 'sunk' in action.

A Draft law was passed. (I never did register for the Draft, being in the Reserves months before there was even talk of a Draft.) Going to the Armory became quite interesting. Word got out that Reservists were exempt from the Draft, and when I appeared in civilian clothes (we kept our uniforms in lockers in the Armory), I was greeted with howls to get to the back of the line! Looking back, I saw I had passed a two-block-long line of civilians waiting to enlist. Turning, I said, "I am an officer and I have a good memory for faces. [I wish I did.] If I hear any more, I will remember who you are." Silence reigned.

About this time, Reserve officers with temporary commissions like mine began receiving letters from the Navy Bureau of Personnel (BUPERS) stating, "Apply for active duty. If accepted, your probation will only last one year instead of two. The correspondence course would be waived. Unfortunately, it may take months for your application to be accepted. If accepted, you would be assigned to a shore base to replace a Regular Navy officer, who would then be able to get sea duty." These letters began to sound attractive. I had broken up with my lovely girlfriend, Barbara Washburn. She was so clever, very intelligent, and with a great command of words. Could it be because she was a cousin of Thornton Wilder? We were engaged to marry, but serious quarrels, mostly about her smoking, which she took up after our engagement ("You can't tell _me_ what to do!"), caused too big a rift to heal. I was at loose ends, romantically. None of the other girls I began dating were equal to Barbara. So, I applied for active duty, expecting a several month's wait. Surprise! Within two weeks, I reported for duty aboard the light cruiser **U.S.S. Brooklyn**, CL-40, at Long Beach, California!

Before I left for active duty, Alex Hussey, a Hawaiian and fellow engineer in the Commonwealth Edison Company in Chicago, gave me an address and a phone number. "You might get to Pearl Harbor. If you do, look up my brother, Sam, in Honolulu." I thanked him, but thought, "Honolulu. I've heard of that place, but where the heck is Pearl Harbor? Sounds romantic."

Figure 3, Brand New Ensign, R.E.Cragg

6
Hello, U.S.S. Brooklyn

Mr. Cragg, have you had sea duty?" It was night, and the **Brooklyn** was steaming north along the California coast on the way to San Francisco Bay and the Mare Island Navy Yard. Captain W.W. Smith had invited the two or three newly-arrived Ensigns to his cabin to get acquainted over dinner. "Captain, I don't know if it could be called sea duty. It was really lake duty. It was on Lake Michigan for Reserve training." "Oh," said Captain Smith, "and what sort of a ship were you in?" "An old gunboat," I replied. "She is the **Wilmington**, out of Cleveland. I was throttle-man on the port engine." "*Wilmington!*" Captain Smith exclaimed with excitement. "I was in her when she took the greatest list any U.S. Navy ship ever took without capsizing!" He went on to describe how the ship lay on its side at a 90 degrees list, dead in the water, fires out, and in the center of a fierce typhoon in the China Sea. I told him I had heard the story when it was told to us by the Regular Navy hands, and that we Reservists found it hard to believe that any ship could survive such punishment. Captain Smith said, "Well, you can believe it now. We had a terrible time getting her back up. The fires were put out when the seas poured down the stack. Re-lighting them with wet coal took great ingenuity on the part of the 'black gang'. Talking about coal, did you still get a dirty mess when you were coaling?" I replied that **Wilmington** was now an oil burner, and not even coal dust remained in her empty bunkers.

Orders to active duty had come to my home in Chicago. I was to proceed to San Pedro, California, and report for duty on board the light cruiser,[11] **U.S.S. Brooklyn – CL-40.** I had read about the **Brooklyn**, first built of the Kellogg Peace Pact 10,000 ton cruisers.[12] Constructed in the Brooklyn Navy Yard, she was commissioned in 1937. In order to get maximum firepower, despite her restricted size, fifteen 6-inch guns were crammed onto her decks in five three-gun turrets. Usually turrets are arranged with number two turret high enough that its guns can swing above number one turret. Three turrets forward presented a problem. Number three turret, if higher than number two, would block the view ahead from the bridge. An ingenious design solved this problem. Since the main battery of a ship never fires straight ahead, but to the side,[13] using the roll of the ship to absorb the recoil, number three turret could be made the same height as number one, and swung to either side for firing.

An odd-appearing feature resulted – the secured (at rest) position of number three turret. Its guns could not point forward; they would hit number two. So they were pointed aft. It looked as if number three was aiming at the ship itself.

---

[11] The difference between light and heavy cruisers is not their respective weights. A light cruiser is armed with 6-inch guns, usually with self-contained cartridge ammunition. A heavy cruiser mounts 8-inch guns. Heavy cruisers, borrowing the **Brooklyn** hull design, only had room for a battery of nine guns in three turrets.

[12] For more about the Kellogg Peace Pact, see Appendix 2: *Salmon O. Levinson.*

[13] This was tried once, and once only. The cruiser **Augusta**'s superstructure was shoved aft several feet. Major repairs were needed.

(see Figure 4.) Odd looking or not, it worked. There were many ships of the **Brooklyn** class built. First of its class and built to get the most out of the treaty restrictions, the **Brooklyn** was a favorite of President Franklin D. Roosevelt, who authorized its design long before the country could afford its construction. Perhaps because of the President, **Brooklyn** was sent on unusual voyages.

The **Brooklyn** had a surprise 'stinger' in the form of four center-float seaplanes, designated as 'SOC' (standing for "Scout Observation, Curtiss".) These were kept in a large hangar aft of number five turret. The deck slid away to allow the planes to be hoisted to the two catapults, and their wings unfolded. Two of the planes were usually kept on the catapults, ready for launching. The catapults were powered with the 'one-two punch' of a steam piston plus a six-inch blank cartridge. The planes were the 'eyes' of the ship because they could see to the greatest range of our guns. Extremely slow, the **Brooklyn** planes bore the apt insignia of a flying box turtle. It was said their wings would come off if they exceeded the speed of 150 miles per hour in a dive. (How was this determined, I wonder?)

Arriving at San Pedro, I found that the port used for the **Brooklyn** was really Long Beach, south of, but on the same bay as, San Pedro. The **Brooklyn** couldn't even be seen from San Pedro! However, my chest, with my uniforms, had been sent to San Pedro. (Why did the Navy make this mistake?) After getting to Long Beach and reporting to the **Brooklyn**, I had to wear civilian clothes aboard ship until the next day, when I went with a ship's boat to pick up my chest in San Pedro.

The other officers couldn't believe that all I had in the form of uniforms were the three required of a Reserve officer: one blue uniform and two whites. That was all my clothing allowance would provide. The Supply Officer looked it up, and determined I was entitled to enough additional clothing allowance to buy more uniforms. There wasn't enough time to rectify this shortcoming before we left for San Francisco Bay and the Mare Island Navy Yard, but, as soon as I could, I made bus trips from Mare Island Navy Yard to San Francisco for extra uniforms.

It was eerie passing through the Golden Gate at night in a dense fog. Radar was not installed yet, but the Navigator did a wonderful job. I learned later that **Brooklyn** hit an entrance buoy there on a previous occasion, bending about six feet of waterline armor plating outward, making an embarrassing swirl on that side. One reason for the Navy Yard visit was to cut off that projection, which still left ample armor.

While in dry dock in the Mare Island Navy Yard, I was sleeping in the cooler upper bunk when I dreamed a devil was casting sparks of fire on me! Holes were being bored in the deck here and there to install some of the things added to us in the Yard. Hot steel shavings had dropped on me when a large drill chewed through the armor of the deck right above me. I quickly transferred to the lower bunk! Having no cabin-mate was lucky in this case. Smart officers, who could afford it, lived ashore during this smelly, noisy ordeal, which went on, day and night. I wished I could have done the same. There was nothing for an engineer to do at first, all machinery being shut down. A ship out of water is as helpless and pitiful as a stranded whale, and it soon began to smell as bad (due to the scrapings from the hull lying rotting on the dry-dock floor.) Suddenly, however, there was plenty for me to do, and Navy Yard life became fun.

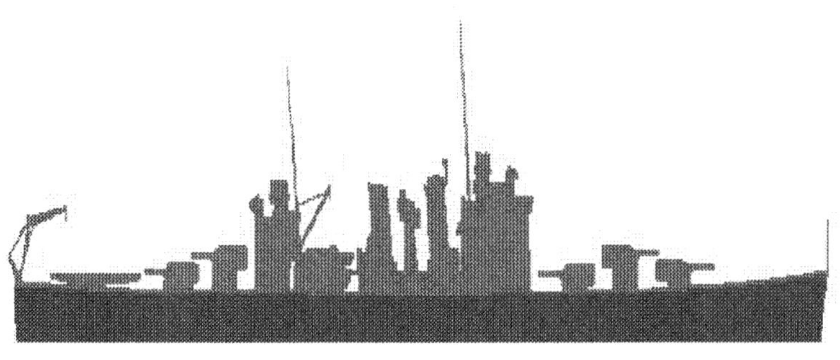

Figure 4. U.S.S. Brooklyn CL-40   USN Archives

Figure 5. The above picture was taken before **Brooklyn**'s sojourn in Mare Island Navy Yard, where gun tubs were built around the eight 5" dual-purpose guns (surface and air). It was also taken prior to the welding over of the portholes, 'perpetrated' in Pearl Harbor by the fleet tender **U.S.S. Antares**.   Jesse P. Mannix photo

7

The 'Wild Gauss Chase'

Phew, what an awful stink! Poor **Brooklyn** is out of her element. High and dry and resting on her blocks in dry-dock in the Mare Island Navy Yard,[14] she reeks from the rotting remains of countless barnacles, seaweed, and other 'critters' scraped from her hull and covering the floor of the dock. A new coat of 'non-fouling' plastic bottom paint will now be applied. **Brooklyn** will have two other big jobs done on her, also. Splinter shields (known as 'gun tubs') are to be constructed around all eight deck-mounted 5-inch guns. The British learned in combat that even a 'near miss,' exploding on the surface alongside, can be fatal to the crews of unprotected guns. Fragments of the shell would fly up, but these shields stopped them.

The other major work to be performed is installing 'de-gaussing' cables. As officer in charge of the E-division (electrical), I am ordered to learn all about this 'hush-hush' operation. My schoolroom is the Yard's 'operations shack' (office). Entering the little one-room building, and stating my purpose, I am greeted with, "OK, here's your textbook." I'm given a <u>two-year old copy of *Science and Mechanics*</u>

---

[14] Mare Island Navy Yard is adjacent to Vallejo, California, at the north end of San Francisco Bay.

Magazine, explaining *everything* about the 'secret'. It is their only copy and so, must be read in the shack.

An American invention at the end of World War I, the magnetic mine was perfected by Germany between wars, and used with devastating effect against the British navy and its merchant marine. A large mass of steel, like a ship, attracts and concentrates the Earth's magnetic field. A magnetic mine resting on the bottom in shallow water contains a magnetic needle which, when attracted by the surge of magnetism from a ship passing above it, triggers a compressed air valve. The compressed air, by blowing water out of the mine, causes the mine to rise from the bottom. At a preset depth, the mine explodes right under the hull (where there is no armor), probably sinking the ship.

Recalling grammar school Science class, wrapping a coil of wire around a piece of iron or steel, and passing electric current from a battery through the coil, turns the steel into a magnet. British scientists wrapped an entire ship in a huge coil and passed current through the coil to turn the ship into a magnet opposing the Earth's magnetic field. The ship's magnetic influence is neutralized just as if the ship were not there. This procedure counters the Earth's magnetism, which is measured in Gausses, so the procedure became known as 'de-gaussing'.

The de-gaussing coils were installed, and connected to a switchboard in the forward engine room where there was a direct current generator to power the coils. Ships are uneven magnetically, with much more steel amidships than the relatively 'clean' fore and after decks. To counteract this imbalance, coils were necessary around the fore and after decks in addition to the main coil, which went around the whole ship. These three coils each contained multiple coils, controlled by switches, so variable current strengths could be set. Once the coils were in place, they had to be calibrated.

Off the coast of California are several islands, two of which, San Clemente and Santa Catalina, were used for de-gaussing calibration. On the bottom, between these two islands, was placed a magnetic needle which indicated to some British officers (on loan to the United States) on Santa Catalina Island whether we were magnetically 'neutral' or not. The **Brooklyn** is long, and the way it was facing relative to the Earth's field made a difference in the magnetic influence it had on the calibrating needle. We went back and forth over the needle in many directions, changing coil currents as dictated by radio. I was on the bridge, connected by JV phone (sound powered headset) to the engine room switchboard, relaying the switch settings to the Electrician's Mate.

After the calibration, I was furnished with a formula to determine the switch settings for the three coils for every ten degrees of steering anywhere in the world. The Earth's variable field strength, direction, and slant, all of which were provided in the ship's navigation charts, were to be inserted in the equation. This meant I had to be on the bridge when the ship was in shallow water (under 30 fathoms) to give the switchboard operator new switch settings whenever we made a turn. This was no hardship in the Pacific Ocean, which is quite deep except near land.

At this time, I requested that a protective grating be placed around the exposed high voltage connections at the back of the de-gaussing switchboard. Lieutenant Commander Herring, 'First Lieutenant' (third in command under the Captain and the Executive Officer, and responsible for the ship's expenditures) refused to allow this expense. A serious consequence of Mister Herring's penny-pinching decision will be demonstrated in Chapter 19. He could well have cost the ship!

Immediately after the incorporation of the de-gaussing coils, the **Brooklyn** received an imperative request from Admiral H.E. Kimmel,[15] commander of Cruiser Division 8 (CRUDIV 8), four cruisers of the **Brooklyn** class.[16] Worried about where the de-gaussing cables passed through decks, bulkheads, and armor possibly resulting in weak spots, Kimmel wanted a description from each ship in his command as to where penetrations were cut. The job was turned over to me, of course, for who else would know? Fresh from the Commonwealth Edison Company in Chicago, where I had been doing a lot of drafting, I drew a plan of the **Brooklyn**. All the cables visible on deck were drawn with bold solid lines. When they disappeared to run below decks, they were drawn with bold dotted lines. The frame and deck numbers where openings had been cut were lettered alongside.

Admiral Kimmel liked the way I did it. He sent all the other reports back to be re-done like mine. I should have received a commendation. The Executive Officer, F.C. Denebrink, properly should have told Mr. Cavenagh, Chief Engineer, who then would have told me. Please note that Commander Denebrink didn't like Reservists (I was the only Reserve officer aboard at the time except for the aviators), and he didn't like Engineering Duty Only (EDO) officers — and I was both! I believe Denebrink resented the fact that the Academy bred E-division officers (*all full Lieutenants and two ranks higher*) in our sister ships were required to resubmit their reports *a la* Reservist Ensign (EDO) Cragg. Kimmel's praise of my report was related to me by my Chief Warrant Electrician, Mr. Koon. He had heard about it from

---

[15] Admiral Husband E. Kimmel was promoted on Feb. 1, 1941, over the heads of 37 other Admirals, to be Commander in Chief of the United States Fleet (CINCUS.) Kimmel took our kind Captain, W.W. (Poco) Smith, to be his Chief of Staff.
[16] **Brooklyn** CL-40, **Philadelphia** CL-41, **Savannah** CL-42, and **Nashville** CL-43.

his Warrant Officer counterparts in the other **Brooklyn**s. They, ex-enlisted men all, thought it was hilarious. [17]

It's funny, considering Denebrink's snobbish attitude, how the other 'trade school' (Naval Academy) graduates aboard treated me as if I was one of their own. A bunch of us used to go hiking in the wild wooded trails above Aiea landing in Pearl Harbor (you should see all the houses there now) and in other places, like Samoa and Tahiti, instead of getting 'smashed' at the officers' club.

---

[17] In the summer of 1943, I met Mr. Koon again. I was glad to see that he was now a full Lieutenant while I was still an Ensign. In the **Brooklyn** days, as a Chief Warrant Officer, he ranked 'with and below' an Ensign. His many years of service counted. He was given the rank commensurate with all the pay raises through the years (known as 'fogey') which was good news, for he was a good friend. What a great guy to pass me the good word back then.

8
Hawaii

"Come up on deck and smell the flowers!" said Bob Woodall. But I didn't need to go 'topside'; the aroma was being blown into our cabin impelled by the air scoop protruding from our porthole. I went up to see, and there on the horizon was a little dark speck, the island of Oahu. The air, perfumed with the smell of vegetation and flowers, was coming to us across miles of ocean from that tiny dark shape.

Ensign Robert Woodall, of Chapel Hill, North Carolina, became my cabin mate. With the calibration of the de-gaussing coils completed, **U.S.S. Brooklyn** returned to Long Beach, where Woodall reported for duty. Since I had prior possession of the lower bunk, 'Woody' used the upper. There was a desk apiece, so I kept the one I had already filled.

Woody was a brand new Ensign, a 'ninety day wonder' graduate of the Navy's V-12 program which produced Navy officers (with no sea duty) after three months of study at various colleges. In Long Beach, the **Brooklyn** received a quantity of V-12 graduates whose names all began with W (except for Brekke; misfiled?). There was Wilson, Wakefield, Wasarhaley, Woodall, Wickham, and so on[18].

---

[18] (but no Wiley – see Dedications.)

Out on the Pacific, where the water had the look of opaque light blue paint except up close, we steamed to the west towards Hawaii in company with our flagship **U.S.S. Philadelphia,** CL-41. The flying fish were fun to watch. Having only heard about them, I was amazed to see the great distances they could fly in their desperate attempts to escape some underwater menace, probably a porpoise. As for the porpoises, they loved to swim just inches ahead of our sharp bow, though we were steaming at 18 knots (roughly 21 miles per hour.) With incredible speed, they would dart off to the side, only to return a little later after eating a flying fish or something.

Admiral Kimmel, then-commander of CRUDIV 8, was in his flagship **Philadelphia**, which was fitted with an Admiral's stateroom. The **Brooklyn**, designated as the Division's auxiliary flagship, had an identical stateroom, left vacant, but kept scrupulously clean. If the **Philadelphia** became untenable as the flagship, due to combat damage, or just during Navy Yard repairs, the Admiral would transfer his flag to the **Brooklyn.**

Admiral Kimmel, a Protestant, had the Division Chaplain, a Presbyterian Minister, in his flagship. The auxiliary Division Chaplain, Padre[19] Manion, was aboard the **Brooklyn**, where, every Sunday, one of the compartments was decorated with colorful signal flags fastened to the 'bulkheads' (walls) and furnished with folding chairs to serve as the chapel for the Padre's disrespectfully-called 'magic show'.

On one somber occasion, Padre Manion's services were required in the **Philadelphia** to administer the last rites to a dying sailor. In one of our motor whaleboats (sharp on each end, and most seaworthy of the boats), Padre Manion

---

[19] Navy chaplains are all called 'Padre', even the Rabbis! Manion was a genuine Padre, being Roman Catholic.

was taken across scary seas to make the risky boarding of the other ship.

Another, more pleasant, occasion was Thanksgiving, with turkey and 'the works' served to all hands. The turkey had been carried frozen from California, and stored in the vast freezer locker[20].

Never having been aboard ship, Woody was grateful for the tips passed on by 'Old Navy' Ensign, Dick Cragg. For instance, I advised him never to let Mess-Attendant Coley polish his sword. Once the lacquer is off, a sword must be regularly polished from then on, to prevent rust. We didn't object to his daily polishing of our shoes.

Closing in on Oahu, the *real* 'Old Navy' hands loved to point out sights of interest. Rounding Diamond Head, an extinct volcano, we passed Waikiki Beach and Honolulu. Called to the engine room as we neared the entrance to Pearl Harbor, I tore myself away from the beautiful sight of the wildly verdant mountains and valleys of Oahu. "Ahead half-speed, reverse full-speed, stop"; such orders from the bridge were followed on the four engines as the ship approached its mooring. Finally the order was given, "Shut down all engines," and we were free to leave our stations. I remembered that same order in Grand Traverse Bay in the **Wilmington**, only then it was, "Shut down *both* engines."

Coming topside, I saw we were moored fore-and-aft between two big buoys. Three ships were 'nested' side by side, moored to the same buoys with 'fenders' (large cushions) between ships. **Helena** was next to us, with **Philadelphia** on the other side of **Helena**. Brows were rigged from ship to ship to allow passing between ships. To go ashore from **Helena,** the **Brooklyn** had to be crossed. Looking around, I saw other three-cruiser 'nests' near us in

---

[20] Instead of burial at sea, the sailor who died was kept in the **Philadelphia**'s freezer awaiting burial in Hawaii.

Pearl Harbor. Here we are, Pearl, end of this leg of our journey.

Figure 6, Whites for Hawaii

9
The Hussey Family

"You are invited to a 'baby luau'? How could that happen? You've only been here two weeks. I've been here three years, but the only luaus I have ever gone to were the commercial ones put on by hotels. How did you get in on something where only Hawaiians are welcome?" The **Brooklyn** officers and their wives were having a party celebrating our return from the mainland. Mrs. Cavenagh, the Chief Engineer's wife, was asking the questions. If I had known it was so special, I would have kept silent about the luau, especially to my boss's wife.

At the first chance I had after reaching Hawaii, I went to Honolulu. Arriving in Honolulu after car-pooling in a cab from Pearl (the customary practice, I found), I called Sam Hussey. "Where are you? I'll come and pick you up." This was my introduction to the most hospitable people I have ever known. Once I arrived at their house, the Husseys proceeded to make me practically part of their family. They insisted I must stay with them whenever I was on overnight leave from the **Brooklyn**, or, if just for the day, I must spend it with them while they acquainted me with Hawaii.

Sam Hussey, brother of fellow engineer Alex Hussey at the Edison Company in Chicago, a graduate of William and Mary College, and a World War I veteran,[21] with his wife, Konda, had room for me in spite of all who lived with them. Their three teenagers were Sam Jr., daughter Anne Leilani (a world-class swimmer known as 'Lani'), and Cynthia, a blue eyed blonde. Konda's mother, Bernice Van Giessen, a lovely lady with regal bearing, also lived with them. Cynthia's blonde coloration came from 'haole' (Caucasian) blood, both in the Hussey ancestry, and from the late Mr. Van Giessen.

Friends of the Husseys were having a luau celebrating the birth of a grandchild. I was invited, as was my **Brooklyn** cabin mate Bob Woodall, who shared some of the Hussey hospitality with me. This luau was the real thing! For instance, entertainment was not provided by 'entertainers'; instead, the guests brought their guitars, their ukuleles, and their drums and played while other guests sang and danced the hula. Sam Hussey 'cut' a mean hula, believe me! A tourist could not have been at this occasion at any price!

Food was plentiful! Servings of pork were carved from the 'umu' pig exhumed from an earthen oven. A deep pit (umu) had been dug in the ground and thoroughly lined with 'ti' leaves (long and wide). The hefty pig, with body cavity filled with hot lava rocks and wrapped in ti leaves, was buried for hours in the *umu* until its meat was succulent and juicy. In the *umu* were included many leaf wrapped packets holding vegetables or fish. When opened, the packets gave forth a delicious, steamy aroma foretelling the exquisite taste of the contents. On the tables were finger foods such as tiny dried and salted shrimp, to be eaten whole like popcorn, which they resembled. The shells of such immature shrimp

---

[21] Sam suffered from severe asthma, a reminder of the unhealthy trench warfare in the 'War to End All Wars.' Sometimes at night he would wake up choking; vapors from burning medicinal herbs gave some relief.

were thin and crunchy when eaten, which heightened their resemblance to popcorn.

Though the only pure *haoles* there, Woody and I were made very much at home. Across the table sat two or three venerable Hawaiian women who conversed with us, but every so often talked to each other in Hawaiian. What a pleasure to hear this musical language spoken. Sam told us later they were discussing Woody and me and thought we were handsome! How about that! What a party it was!

The Husseys and their cousins were well known and respected. Sam was head of the citric acid refining department at Dole's Hawaiian Pineapple Company and Konda supervised its huge international switchboard. A niece, Bernice Van Giessen, a breathtakingly beautiful young woman, was head of Dole's pretty guides who, wearing beanies resembling pineapples, escorted visitors through the plant. (I had a special guided tour, just for me.) After Bernice had been elected Hawaii's 'Pineapple Queen' three times, she refused to run again, in spite of heavy company pressure, saying it had become embarrassing. She later married a fine young man named Matson to whom she was engaged when I was there.

The Husseys used their precious gasoline, imported from the mainland, to take me sightseeing. Konda, especially, was eager to educate me about Hawaiian flora. I learned about kukui nuts, which, when polished a shiny black, were strung on leis (necklaces). Candlenuts, when pierced and a wick inserted, would burn for a couple of hours from the oil inside. What marvels she showed me!

We went body-surfing in a bay noted for this activity. Much to the Husseys' surprise, I was better at it than they were. After catching a good wave, I could ride it all the way to the beach. After doing what I could with the short lived Lake Michigan waves, surfing these perfect waves proved to be a 'snap'. By the way, and as far as I know, Sam Jr. is the only Hawaiian in history who ever got seasick on a surfboard. His family teased him about it.

On one trip, Sam stopped by an old shack by the sea beyond Diamond Head. In the yard were clotheslines festooned with octopuses drying in the sun. (They call them squids in Hawaii, but they are *not* squids. Squids have ten arms, not eight.) An ancient Hawaiian woman came out to the car to talk to Sam in Hawaiian, and they laughed a lot, glancing occasionally at me. Later, out of family hearing, Sam told me the old woman was wondering how I would be in bed! She was 104 years old then! The Husseys sent me a clipping when she died at 108. This old woman lived alone, subsisting by selling the octopuses she caught after swimming out to the offshore reef. To kill an octopus, one bites out an eye, thus paralyzing the simple nervous system. If one didn't do this, the octopus could hold one under water until drowned. When the octopus had been dried, salted, and sliced like cold cuts, I found it to be delicious and fine exercise for the jaws.

I seldom went back to the **Brooklyn** empty handed. If it wasn't a huge avocado from the avocado base planting around their house, it was a couple of the pineapples specially picked for Dole management. These were unavailable in the store, whose fruits were picked before prime and ripened on the shelf. No - these magnificent pineapples were selected in the field by Dole experts who could tell when they were at their peak of sweetness and juiciness.

I sent a box of these special ones home to Chicago by Pan American Clipper. $10 to ship eight, which was expensive back then, but well worth it. Those pineapples lasted longer than mine did once the fellows from Annapolis found out I had them. "You can't eat that whole thing by yourself!" I did better with the avocados with lemons I took from the galley.

On another day, we all went to the big saltwater swimming pool by the sea where Lani was competing in a world championship qualification meet. Lani was well ahead of everyone when suddenly she pulled over to the side of the pool. By the time we got to her, she had been hauled out and was in intense pain. At the hospital, it turned out she had appendicitis and her appendix had ruptured while she was swimming. She recovered after an appendectomy, but her chance at a world title had to be forgotten indefinitely.

10

Advice to New Officers

"Hey you! – – There's smoke coming out."

"No s . . t! Where?"uttered Jake while answering the phone call from the bridge.

"Wait a minute; I'll look . . . . It's behind me near the back chimney."

"OK, I'll look into it."

"Dick, go topside and see what's going on!" said Ensign Arnold Jaeckel. "OK, Jake." I replied. When I arrived on deck and looked aft, there was only a faint wisp of smoke coming from the galley stack – not an abnormal event – seen whenever a batch of something or another got burnt in cooking. The cooks told me they had burned some loaves of bread – no problem. I reported this to Jake when I returned to the forward engine room – that it was just ordinary 'Charley Noble' (galley stack) smoke and of no consequence.

Jake called the bridge and asked for the officer who called the engine room about the smoke. The officer turned out to be one of the newly arrived '90-day wonders', obnoxious Ensign Wilson from New York City. He was assured there was no danger to the ship, there was no violation of the 'no smoke on the horizon' ship's regulation, and no action would be taken. *And then Jake 'went to town!'*

"I am the '**bull Ensign**' (most senior) in this ship!" he roared into the phone! "You had better find out what that means, and change your attitude. Somewhere you got the idea that everyone in the engine room is inferior to you because you are a *deck* officer." [He might have absorbed this idea from Commander Denebrink whose distaste for engineering was obvious.] "Well, you came close to being put on report for disrespect to an officer senior to you. How would you like to appear at Captain's Mast (deck trial) tomorrow morning?" Jake turned to me and gave a 'thumbs down' sign, and held his nose in disgust. "Pass the word around among the other 90-day wonders what nearly happened to you. I will not tolerate any more 'Hey yous' from you, and any other disrespect by *any of you* to engine room personnel, whether we are officers or enlisted men, *will result in the offender being put on report!"* [Well said, Jake!]

Ensign Jaeckel, Naval Academy graduate, and absorbed with the **Brooklyn** engineering plant, was teaching me how to stand engine room watches. He was delighted when he got a graduate Engineer for an associate. Clad in dungarees and grungy officer's hats, we explored the entire ship below decks. We gave **Brooklyn**'s laundry a lot of greasy business.

I learned that fuel oil at ordinary temperatures was about as fluid as molasses. To move it to the burners in the fire rooms, it must be heated to the 'flash point' – that temperature at which it will spontaneously burn if sprayed into the air. Then it is quite fluid and can be pumped. I learned that exhaust steam, even after losing much heat in driving the big turbines, was still hot enough to heat the oil using steam coils inside the oil 'voids' (tanks formed by the space between the inner and outer hulls). Enough heat was left in the exhaust steam to boil saltwater in the evaporators used to distill the water for shipboard use. The used steam was hot enough to cook, fry, bake, and even to burn a batch of bread.

We went down into 'steering aft' where the steam powered steering engine pistons were located. To get there required descending a vertical shaft from the hangar deck to way below the waterline and just forward of the rudder. There were two men on watch there at all times when the ship was at battle stations. If the control cables from the bridge were cut, these men, with sound powered phones (in case of power failure to the phone system), would assume 'local control' of the steering engine and follow the steering orders from the bridge. In case of loss of steam to the steering engine, there was a system of gears in steering aft for manually cranking the rudder. The Machinist's Mates assigned to this station were big and brawny on purpose. I did not envy them - steering aft is very confined. To 'fast forward' a bit, the German battleship, **Bismarck,** was doomed when her steering area was hit, causing her to steam in circles. Imagine the state in *her* steering aft at that time!

Jake showed me places that Commander Denebrink wouldn't know, nor would that 'Wilson wonder' from the bridge. Jake showed me how to escape from the engine room should it be flooded. There was an enclosed shaft in each engine room with a ladder, not one of those stairs which are called ladders on board ship, but a real vertical ladder with rungs, not stair steps. This ended in a watertight hatch, dogged down from the main deck, but unsealing also from below. Once in a while we left the engine room by that route at the end of our watch, just for practice. Many a deck hand was startled when we emerged on deck from a hatch they hadn't really noticed before except to swab around and keep painted.

Ensign Jaeckel, to Denebrink's disgust I'm sure, had applied for Engineering Duty Only status, and was granted his request. In late April, after returning from a long voyage, he said goodbye, and left the **Brooklyn** for graduate school at MIT. I sure did miss my good friend, the 'bull Ensign'.

My advice to new officers? Be polite to people on the phone. You never know when rudeness will do you harm; or you could be talking to the Captain (on the phone or at Mast).

11
A Christmas to Remember

"I'd like to go to church," said Woody. Straight from the 'bible belt' state of North Carolina,[22] Ensign Bob Woodall had gone to church every Christmas Day of his life. Always obliging, Konda Hussey went to the phone to find a church with services at that late hour of the morning. We hadn't arrived at the Husseys until 10 AM. The red tape of leaving the **Brooklyn**, plus competing in the mad scramble for a cab, followed by the miles to Honolulu, took time. Konda finally found a church with services at 11 AM. I don't recall the denomination, but this didn't matter to Bob. The Husseys, casual Catholics, seldom went to church, and I, an ecumenical type, didn't care.

Our group was elegant, particularly Grandmother Bernice Van Giessen, in her formal *muumuu* (long Hawaiian gown), and her beautiful white hair piled high on her head.

---

[22] It was interesting how Southerner Bob Woodall warmed up to the Husseys. At first quite reserved, he began to understand these people were not 'natives,' but were cultured, well educated, and so very friendly! Civilized? Oh, my! Konda would not let Sam Jr. and me go barefoot around the house as we wanted. She said she wanted no 'kanakas' (literally, 'dog eaters,' a derogatory term referring to a low type of Hawaiian) around *her* house!

Proudly, our party entered the church, only to have the quietly playing organ interrupted by a blast – *from under my feet*! In Hawaii, as in parts of the south, it is customary to shoot off fireworks at Christmas. Someone had put a 'torpedo' under the openwork aisle carpet, and it was my misfortune to step on it. There I was, smoke wreathing around my legs, the subject of indignant glares from the congregation. I was obviously guilty. I wished I could disappear.

My embarrassment was not over. The congregation's disapproval resumed when a lengthy string of firecrackers began exploding right outside the building. We heard the progress of the explosions as they slowly circled the church. I must, of course, be responsible for this sacrilege too. Thankfully, Woody and I were not in uniform, it being peacetime. No complaints would reach the **Brooklyn**. There was only one bright note in this whole episode: the long, boring, droning sermon was inaudible due to the racket outside. Through it all, Mrs. Van Giessen retained her dignity.

Back home at the Husseys, we were recovering from that ordeal, only to find ourselves in another one. Bob and I each made a serious mistake that day. Mine was to contribute a bunch of skyrockets, while Woody had brought Sam some liquor from the officers' club at Pearl Harbor. Konda was upset with both of us, for she knew what was going to happen. Booze, skyrockets, and Hawaiians are an exciting mix! Sam had never had anything bigger than firecrackers before, so, when darkness fell and Sam saw what rockets could do, he grabbed all of them. When he began trying to hit Sam Kahanamoku's house across the street,[23] Bob and I

---

[23]The Hussey's friend, Sam Kahanamoku, was Doris (richest girl in the world) Duke's estate caretaker. His brother, Duke Kahanamoku, was the fastest Olympic swimmer in the world. Brother Dave was an officer in the Hawaiian National Guard.

watched in horror as the rockets went screaming off Sam K.'s roof. We could see the family peering fearfully out their windows at the scary stream of fiery missiles whizzing at them from across the street. Bob and I were expecting the police to arrive momentarily. Suppose Sam K's house caught fire! Bob and I would be caught like rats in a trap! We were staying the night and couldn't escape. We had visions of a General Court Martial with us as the defendants. Reserve officers would not fare well in the peacetime Navy.

Finally, thank Heavens, Sam ran out of skyrockets! Then Sam Kahanamoku and his family came over. There was much hilarity, and Sam K. said it was the most fun Christmas ever. The two Sams finished the liquor, and all was friendly and nice – except for Konda, who wouldn't speak to us. On the way back to the **Brooklyn** the next day, Bob declared he would not bring Sam any more bottles, to which I replied, "Amen." Thus ended a rare Christmas, and one never to forget!

12
Millions for the Asking

While I was going up the walk to spend my overnight leave from the **Brooklyn** with the Husseys in their Honolulu home, I met a man coming down the walk cursing loudly and fluently as he strode angrily along. He was obviously 'mainland' since he was wearing a suit with coat and tie. "What was that all about?" I asked the family. "Oh, that was just another of those lawyer pests from New York," was their answer.

The Husseys told this strange story. The New York World's Fair of 1939 had been located on Native American tribal land, with no permission asked or granted. The last surviving member of that tribe, or nation, was now Grandmother Bernice Van Giessen. Many New York lawyers, smelling money, found which nation had 'title' to that land. One by one, they had traced it from New York, through Oklahoma, to Hawaii, and there they found our tribal princess, living with her daughter's family, the Husseys.

Native American nations were not used to recognizing land as an entity to be owned, but United States law did! (Things have changed recently.) New York had trespassed on tribal land, rent-free, and left trash and trashy buildings behind. Recompense in the order of many millions of dollars was due the nation, which was now solely Grandmother Van Giessen. All she had to do was sign some claim papers, and she would be very, very rich! Grandmother refused to sign, saying her life was beautiful and happy, and she wanted to keep it that way.

One after another, the lawyers went swearing down that walk, starting their long and fruitless voyage back to the mainland. Years later, when asked if he regretted his grandmother's decision not to sign, Sam Hussey, Jr. (now a graduate of Northwestern University and a statistician with a prominent ratings company) told me, "No, she was right. It would have ruined our lives." (The lawyers would have done all right, however!)[24]

I had to learn more about this intriguing woman. What was the Bernice Van Giessen story? I found out she had a fascinating life. Her father, Chief and sole survivor of his Native American nation, brought her to Hawaii from Oklahoma during the reign of Queen Liliuokalani, feeling she would have a richer life. He was absolutely right! Attractive Bernice soon became popular at court and was appointed Lady-in-Waiting to the Queen. She told me amusing tales of the royal babies, who, sensing at an early age that they were special, could be very demanding.

The Chief bequeathed his house to his daughter, where she entertained some illustrious guests. When Robert Louis Stevenson visited Hawaii, he always boarded at her house. "What was he like?" I asked. She told me he was quite frail, and he really enjoyed the hot soups she made for him. He felt they were good for him.

It was easy to see how she became so well-liked at court. Personally attractive as I knew her, and with dignified bearing, she was also a Princess in her own right. If her granddaughter, Bernice was any indication, she must have

---

[24]"Ownership of land is, at best, a useful human fiction." *Anonymous.*

been a 'knockout' indeed! What a privilege it was for me to
know this unique lady and hear her stories. I termed her my
'Princess at the Palace.'

13
Arming Midway Island – 1941

The Admiral[25] is fuming mad! Even though he used extraordinary means to conceal the manning and fortification of that great ring of coral called Midway Island, it was no use. All Hawaii was talking about it when we returned. The Admiral says there are too many leaks, and he wants them stopped. I have my doubts – is it possible to seal a sieve?

From bulkhead-to-bulkhead (wall-to-wall) folding cots filled the spacious below deck hangar in the high speed light cruiser **U.S.S. Brooklyn,** a favorite of Franklin D. Roosevelt's who authorized its heavily armed 'pact beating' design years before she could be built[26]. To make room for the cots, the four scout planes were hoisted out of the hangar at night and stored on the catapults. As **Brooklyn** sortied from Pearl Harbor before sunrise, 500 Marines were below in those cots and the hangar deck closed tight over them after they secretly boarded that night. Ensign Cragg remembers all the secrecy well, though stationed in the engine room, for getting underway at night in peacetime was most unusual. Until we were out of sight of land, the Marines were kept hidden below and invisible. This was the 'extraordinary

---

[25]Admiral Husband E. Kimmel.
[26]See Appendix 2 - Salmon O. Levinson

means' of the Admiral; for no observer, seeing us leave, would guess that a small army was going to sea hidden in the **Brooklyn**. After all, **Brooklyn** is a sleek cruiser, not a transport ship. A transport would be too obvious–a dead giveaway of the secret.

When well at sea, we passed five cargo ships going the same direction. 'Scuttlebutt' (rumor) in the **Brooklyn** had it the ships were loaded with heavy artillery, both surface and anti-aircraft. Scuttlebutt also had it that ammunition ships would follow later.

After we steamed west for a thousand miles, I saw my first tropical atoll, Midway Island. Nobody knew in February 1941 that just over a year later Midway would be the focus of the most pivotal battle of the WW II Pacific Theater.

Picture a coral reef five miles in diameter enclosing a lagoon[27]. At its eastern edge is a narrow channel, turning sharply to the left just inside the reef. Out of this channel a current is always flowing. Waves break over the opposite or western wall of the coral ring, and all the added water exits through this one vent. Inside the lagoon, on each side of the channel, lies an island. The larger island (Sand Island), to the left of the channel, has docking for large ships, like the **Brooklyn**, as well as fuel tanks, buildings, and an airstrip. There are trees. The right hand arid Bird Island, later named East Island, has swarms of birds continually circling. A year later, an airstrip and other construction had been added. One wonders what happened to all the 'gooney' birds – a hazard to the Navy and Marine aviators who heroically took off from that runway to help devastate a Japanese fleet.

Our 500 Marines are to be released from their cramped quarters in the **Brooklyn** and landed on the dock on

---

[27]Pan-American Airways landed its 'Manila Clippers' in the smooth waters of the Midway lagoon for fueling en-route to the Orient after fueling in Pearl Harbor, where they landed in the West Loch.

Sand Island. Recently there had been strong winds and huge seas, breaking over the western reef, causing high water inside the lagoon. The outflow, now a raging torrent, was too strong for the **Brooklyn**. She could not negotiate the sharp turn without being bashed into the coral. The Marines had to be unloaded promptly before we ran out of food. **Brooklyn** had to wait outside the reef, but her small boats, due to their shortness, were capable of transiting the channel, making the turn easily. Boatload after boatload, the 500 Marines were taken through the channel to be landed on Sand Island. The other ships could wait offshore. (Artillery and ammunition eat nothing.) The **Brooklyn** returned to Hawaii and Pearl Harbor, but these ships remained for better weather and inside docking to unload their deadly cargoes.

In Honolulu, there was widespread gossip of the 'secret mission' to fortify Midway Island. Perhaps it was even mentioned in *The Honolulu Advertiser*. The next time I had shore leave, my Hawaiian friends, the Husseys, asked, "How was your trip west? Did you go ashore on Midway Island?" My short "No!" was all the answer I gave them. Even to my trusted friends, I saw no need to add to the rumors, those leaks which so enraged Admiral Kimmel. Japanese spies were teeming throughout the islands, even in fishing 'sampans' with short wave radios, and all the precautions, which at times seemed extreme, were actually not enough. If we only knew!

Public knowledge or not, a strong bastion of the United States has been established, far out in the Pacific Ocean. Two-thirds of the way to Japan, Midway backs up the outposts of Guam, Wake Island, and the Philippines, all three of which might be impossible to defend because of their remote locations. Now no secret, fortified Midway Island will have to be reckoned with by our potential foe, Japan.

A year later, the Philippines, Guam, and Wake Island had been lost, but the 'Battle of Midway' in June, 1942 was the turning point of the War in the Pacific. The **Brooklyn** played a proud part in the arming of Midway which made this triumph possible.

14
Storm

Even the **Brooklyn** – President's pet – had to have a storm thrown at her once in a while. (I remembered how the **Wilmington** suffered through a Lake Michigan storm – no laughing matter.) When the wind began blowing, and the seas began rolling, the **Brooklyn** began rolling - and pitching too. How I missed my **Wilmington** hammock in which I felt nothing. The 'nice' inner-spring mattresses so lavishly provided to us officers were not as nice as the stark fold-down firm bunks of the enlisted men. What happens is that one's body sinks into the springy mattress and is rolled in it, first one side, then the other, making for an uncomfortable rest. It kept me awake during the storm, so I did something very unorthodox - I put the mattress on deck athwart-ship (crosswise) so the roll no longer 'rolled' me. Everyone thought I was nuts, but 'don't knock it 'til you've tried it.' The pitching of the ship was inconsequential amidships where my cabin was located; and I had good sleeping.

The Warrant Officers as well as the Chiefs, whose quarters were both located far forward, were uncomfortable in a different respect. When the ship was pitching, to go where they slept was like riding a roller-coaster, with its abrupt plunges and swooping lifts. Once I was a guest of Mr. Koon, Chief Warrant Electrician, at his mess. It was a good thing I have a strong set of sea-legs (and stomach); for the ride was a wild one.

Since we were rolling 30 degrees to each side, the treasurer of the officers' mess decided we would not sit at the tables and be served as usual, but would have cold cuts and salad served buffet style from bowls on the tables while we sat around the edges of the wardroom, just like a shore-side party. This should have worked fine except the roll was too much, and one after another, the bowls slid off the tables and crashed to the deck. Since nobody got hurt, I thought it was funny to see the Mess Attendants sliding from one side to the other on mayonnaise. There was one officer sliding around on his butt too - the mess treasurer who was trying in vain to rescue his 'mess'.

Finally, someone who was an old destroyer hand remembered how they did it in the 'cans'. He told the mess treasurer who told the Chief Mess Attendant (following proper Navy protocol in order of command) to put wet tablecloths on the tables. Nothing slid off the tables after that, and the meal became a success after all.

One of the ninety day wonders didn't show up at this meal - Ensign Wakefield. I was not surprised. Poor Wakefield. I had heard the expression, "green around the gills", and thought it to be merely a saying, - not knowing it described reality. Whenever there was the least rolling, Mr. Wakefield would take, maybe, two or three string beans and a half teaspoon of mashed potatoes. After moving them about a bit on his plate, he would get up with the rest of us and leave without eating a bite. He got a greenish-yellow color under each side of his jaw - the location of his gills, I suppose. I wonder how he would have done in an engine room where seeing the horizon without the X-Ray vision of Superman is impossible. Dramamine had not yet been invented for people like Wakefield.

15
Under Sail in Pearl Harbor

"But Mr. Hanson doesn't do it that way." Mr. Hanson *was a graduate of the **Naval Academy**, and what does a Reserve officer like Mr. Cragg know about sailing? I happened to know a bit more about sailing than most (even Mr. Hanson), having sailed my own 13½ foot sloop **Pollywog** on Lake Michigan since a teenager. I learned some sailing refinements from two able teachers. An early girl-friend, Faraday Benedict (descendant of Sir Michael Faraday, the famous scientist), taught me some basic tricks of her father, Robert P. Benedict, owner of **Bagheera**, a black forty-three foot schooner which had won the famous Mackinac race several times. She taught me, in my own little boat sailing off the beach at Lakeside, Michigan, her father's principle of sail handling – mainly that the sail pulling harder on its controlling sheet because of trimming it in tightly does *not* mean faster sailing, though it feels like it. Slacking off a sail so it almost 'luffs' gets the most out of it. Almost everyone senses the opposite; so I beat 'em. (This principle does not apply to catamarans which sail so fast they generate their own apparent head wind.)

My other 'teacher', Doctor Bob Bigelow, brother of my Purdue classmate Glenn who later introduced Dorothy (my wife to be) and me, had been a sailing instructor at

Indiana's Culver Military Academy. He emphasized that the more upright a sailboat is, the more efficient its sails and centerboard become. Similar to the delusionary pull on the sheet, the more a boat is heeled, the faster it falsely feels. (There is another exception – the Inland Lakes 'Scow' which is designed to sail heeled over.) Bob also told me that the crew, when sitting up high, caught the wind and slowed the boat. I kept my crew concentrated on the windward side with only their heads showing above the rail.

Another trick Dr. Bigelow showed me was an efficient way of jibing. When jibing, as around a marker buoy, instead of hauling in the sheet and letting it out through the pulleys as fast as possible after the jibe – the usual way – instead, grab all parts of the sheet where they pass through the pulleys, and swing the sail across by hand, taking the shock with the arm. This not only saves time, it could prevent a capsize.

The sailing whaleboats carried by cruisers and battleships were twenty-six feet long, double ended with a centerboard, and carrying three sails on two masts. There were two sails of equal size and a jib. I believe this would properly be called a schooner rig. (See Figure 7.) The rudder was outboard and controlled with a tiller. There were two designs of whaleboat in the fleet, an older, broader, and more stable boat, and a much faster and later design with finer lines. The many cruisers in Pearl Harbor all had the faster design except three ships, and **Brooklyn** was one of these three. By my insisting on obedience (no matter how Mr. Hanson might do it), we always beat the other two slow boats and half of the fast ones too in spite of having a slower boat.

Whaleboat races were held in the East Loch of Pearl Harbor. To avoid congestion, boats from the cruisers were raced on Thursdays – the battleship boats on another day of the week. A different division and a different Ensign supplied the crew and skipper each week As I enjoyed sailing, I was happy to take the place of any Ensign who was willing. Most found shore leave preferable, so I sailed a lot. The crews from the deck divisions were the most likely to question the commands of a Reserve – Engineering Duty Only – officer. It usually required argument to get things right at the outset. The 'black gang' divisions – who knew me – did better, but the best crew of all was the Marine division! "All hands to the weather side." Zip – it was done. "All hands down with only heads above the rail." Zip – it was done. "Slack off slightly on the jib." Zip – it was done. We beat more of the faster boats with Marines for a crew than with any other division.

One day, I took the dentist, Doctor L.L. Cross on board for a race. He enjoyed himself thoroughly, having a good knowledge of sailing, but he was never even considered as a skipper – out of character, you know. Besides, what if someone had a tooth-ache while he was out sailing? After the race, on approaching the ship, I turned into the wind so as to stop directly under the boat boom. Doc Cross thought it would show sharp seamanship to drop the sail on our approach, which he did, mashing my hands between the boom and the tiller so I couldn't steer! Also it hurt! My 'cussing' ("Lift the boom, damn it! I can't steer!") was loud enough to cause the Captain to put his head out of his porthole to see what was going on. The boat didn't end up quite where I intended, but close enough that a man in the bow was able to grab one of the lines hanging from the boat boom.

My strength in 1941 was enough that I could climb a line to the boat boom hand-over-hand without using my legs. This feat impressed some, for most had to use the rope ladder, including the dentist – ha, ha!. Times have changed, and so have I. I might have grown old, I think.

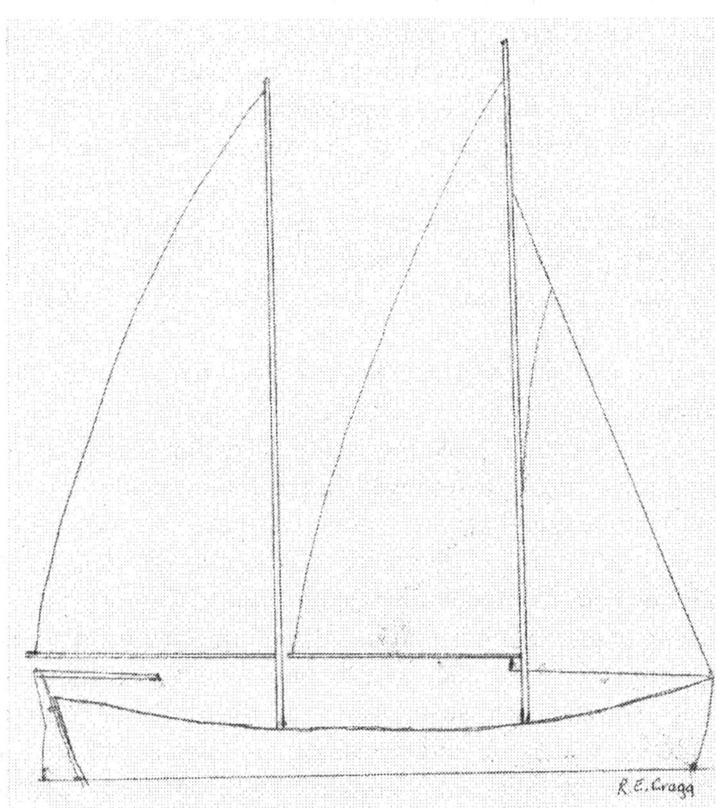

Figure 7, 26' Sailing Whaleboat-as remembered by the author. In *Sailing at the U.S.Naval Academy.* Adm. Robert W. McNitt. Naval Institute Press. Annapolis MD. 1996, the sailing whaleboats are described and illustrated as ketch – not schooner – rigged and 32' – not 26'. I could be wrong after over sixty years, but I think the boats we sailed in Pearl Harbor in 1941 were as I have described them. There were design changes in those years, and the Pearl boats could have differed from the Academy boats.

16
Rest Camp at Nanakuli

"Mr. Cragg, you are to be in charge of the crews from the cruisers going to the rest camp at a place called Nanakuli. You will be gone ten days. Here are your orders to present to the officer in charge. You will take a boat with the **Brooklyn** contingent, land at Pearl City, assemble all hands from the cruisers, and wait for the train for the camp. The battleship crews will be joining you at the train station."

This rest camp had just been written up in the *Honolulu Advertiser*, and I couldn't grasp why I, an Engineering duty only officer, would be picked for this type of duty. It seemed more like a deck officer's sort of job. Nice, sure, but what were my duties? I believe Captain Smith had sized me up from that initial dinner in his quarters and liked what he saw. I think my enlisted experience gave me a bit more 'salt' than was possessed by the new Reserve officers recently assigned to the ship.

The **Brooklyn** boat loaded up with about fifteen men who, properly, went aboard before me. This is to make sure that I, an officer, preceded the enlisted men when debarking.

Not very democratic, but the armed forces cannot be any other way (so I thought until I reached the camp).

There at the Pearl City station was waiting a narrow gauge train with an antique steam locomotive at the head of its train of passenger cars. The cars were ancient day coaches. I talked with the train crew who told us not to board the train until the battleship party joined us. We had about 120 men from the cruisers, but it was a long train with ample seating. The train crew told me the railroad went all over the island of Oahu with many spurs, and was used mainly for transporting sugar cane, but the passenger cars were used for tourist sight-seeing. When visiting Hawaii since the War, I found that trucks now do the sugar cane hauling, and the only passenger train left was on the island of Maui where it runs between Kaanapali and Lahaina.

I did not know what I was supposed to do with all these guys from the cruisers. It seemed silly to form them up into ranks since we had no idea when all the enlisted men from the battleships would be arriving. Besides, I still didn't know how to do it. Also I was in civilian clothes. So - I just didn't do anything.

In about fifteen minutes, an officers' boat pulled up - and two officers in civilian clothes landed, followed by one Mess Attendant struggling with their luggage. "I sure am glad to see you." I said. "Are you in charge of the battleship party?" When they said "Yes," I asked where the battleship party was. "This is it!" they said, pointing to the mess boy. I still don't know the answer, except to guess there must have been a major infraction of the rules just before and some Admiral was terribly peeved. I thought the situation was funny, and sent it in as an anecdote to *The Naval Institute Proceedings* only to get the reply that they were not amused. (I thought Queen Victoria was long dead.)

We all boarded the train, cruiser men and battleship *man*, and the half-empty train chuffed west to the coast, then northerly to the Nanakuli station. The officer in charge (OINC) - dressed in civilian clothes - met us and waved aside my orders. "This place is for rest and relaxation. Those orders don't belong here. I'll sign them just so you have proof that you arrived. There is no rank here either. The uniform of the day is swim wear and you don't even have to wear shoes."

There *was* a difference between officers and enlisted men, in their quarters. The men had six-man huts; the officers were in two-man huts. A hut was just a roof with walls of screen and a wood floor. With such a dearth of officers, I had a hut all to myself, except for its original inhabitants. First I shooed out the centipede - one of those big black shiny ones with orange legs. It looked poisonous, and probably was. Next - out went the scorpion, which I knew darned well was poisonous. The big spider came next. He didn't want to go, so I urged him onto a leaf which I threw out. The lizard I kept. He was my reception committee for any new bugs who might enter.

Rest and relax we did. Contrary to U.S. Navy shipboard rules, beer was plentiful and free. It sure relaxed a lot of guys. I felt somewhat cheated. My view of beer is that I prefer my water *before* it goes through the horse. (Just a relic of Freshman fraternity days - putting beer drunk actives to bed.)

As for swimming, Nanakuli was not an ordinary beach. The waves came in about six or seven feet high, and broke at the very edge of the beach straight down! WHAM! No wading out to where one could swim. To swim, one had to dive straight into this vertical wall of water to arrive on the other side for ordinary swimming conditions. Coming back in was tricky. If one were on top of the wave, one could get hurt falling six or seven feet onto the sand, and some did. No broken bones though. Timing was essential, for between waves there was a chance to get ashore. What I did was swim underwater to come in at the base of the breaker. Sure, I got whacked, but not bad.

Sitting on the beach just watching was fun. A bunch of little Hawaiian kids would lie right where the monster waves landed. It didn't bother them at all to be pounded. Then there were the porpoises. Fantastic swimmers! I saw them come out of the wave wall and go back in before it broke. I'm sure they couldn't have completely emerged into the air - that would be impossible - but it looked that way. I kept expecting one of them to come to grief on the sand, but it never happened. Porpoises seem to me to be the watery equivalent of bungee jumpers, mountain climbers, and other neck-riskers in the human world. I think they have fun.

Ten days of this was enough. How the officer in charge stood it full time, I don't know. He did a great job, for there could have been serious clashes among the men, considering unlimited beer and freedom. There was none of that. (The cruiser men could have easily beaten up the battleship force.) Resting and relaxing for month after month must have been taxing for the OINC, but somebody had to do it.

I feared I would have to make a written report, but Lieutenant Commander Cavenagh, Chief Engineer, just asked me about it - I told him - and that was that.

Nowadays? The rest camp is part of Nanakuli State Park, near the village of Nanakuli. The beach is known as Piliokahe Beach. The meaning of Piliokahe I don't know, but I do know 'pilikia' means danger, and I'll have to ask a Hawaiian to interpret, but I'll bet there is a connection.

17

Introducing Captain Stone

"All hands – man your battle stations!" - - - What is this? How could the **Brooklyn** be going into battle while still moored? It was only 0200 Sunday morning, and the Klaxon alarm was still sounding on the P.A. system as we rushed to our stations. [This was the Spring of 1941, *not* December 7th !] The Warrant Officer Machinist, Mr. Smith, was called on the P.A. to report to the bridge. This was a strange request – made even stranger when soon several Machinist's Mates were also summoned to the bridge. The 'reason' for the call to battle stations was learned only after we were released from combat conditions hours later.

Captain W.W. 'Poco' Smith had been relieved of command of **U.S.S. Brooklyn** in order to become the Chief of Staff to Admiral Husband E. Kimmel, just promoted on February 1 from commanding our small Cruiser Division (CRUDIV8) to become Commander-in-Chief of the entire U.S. Fleet. Captain Ellis S. Stone took over the command of the **Brooklyn** from Captain Smith in a brief ceremony on the quarterdeck. As a perquisite, Captain Stone was issued a new 'gig' (Captain's motorboat) with a powerful, and just re-built, engine. Captain Smith retained his own gig. I have sometimes wondered if Captain Stone was a new Captain, just promoted from Commander after being 'passed over' before, who had never had a gig. He acted like it.

That Saturday night, Captain Stone had been with fellow Captains in the officers' club in Pearl Harbor. Wishing to show off his fast new gig with its powerful engine, he offered rides back to their ships to other Captains, and two or three accepted. On the way, Captain Stone told his Coxswain, "Open her up, son. Let's see what she'll do." So, the Coxswain 'opened her up' – and the clutch burned out! Powerless and adrift in the harbor, vainly hailing liberty boats as they rushed unheedingly past, they spent an hour or more rolling in the wakes of the passing boats until the helpless gig was noticed. A tow was given, first to the other ships to let their Captains off, and then to the **Brooklyn**. How humiliating!

The Captain gave orders to the Officer of the Deck as soon as he came aboard – "Sound General Quarters, and have Mr. Smith report to me on the bridge. Keep everyone at Battle Stations *until my gig is fixed!*" And so we stayed for many hours until the 'All clear' was sounded, presumably after the Machinist and his Mates had repaired or replaced the ailing clutch.

I learned something of comfort during this time – old hands had thoughtfully secreted lidded containers for bladder relief in the engine rooms. We had never been at battle stations this long before. The fire rooms were similarly equipped, but I wondered about the turrets, ammunition handling rooms, and other tight places. 'Steering Aft' would be the worst. It took a 'shoe horn' just to get in there. Oh well, that was their problem. The bridge people made out OK – there was an ever-running urinal right outside the bridge.

This was our introduction to Captain Stone – soon to be 'beloved' by all hands. The already-loved Executive Officer, Commander F.C. Denebrink, was happy, I think – the two talked the same language. Under Captain Smith, the two-cell brig had been kept clean for inspection, but was *never* used. In only one month after the change of command there was a two-month waiting list of Prisoners at Large, wearing a 'PAL' on their uniforms, and restricted to the ship until their jail sentences had been served! None of the Electrician's Mates were ever in that category. I had warned them to be carefully paranoid, and they were. I was proud of them!

18
Pago Pago

Pronounced – believe me – Pango Pango[28]

Left of the entrance to Pago Pago Harbor rises the 'Rainmaker,' the volcanic mountain dramatized in Somerset Maugham's *Rain*. To the right is the height where Robert Louis Stevenson lies buried. Between them, the **Brooklyn** lay at anchor in what is surely the most beautiful harbor in the world. Surrounding us on the tranquil water, good looking Samoans in outrigger canoes sang to us in sweet harmony. Beyond the officers' club lay the town of Pago Pago. The houses ('fales' pronounced fahlays) were from my dreams of the South Seas. Thatched roofs seemed to float airily on circles or rectangles of sturdy posts. No walls were present. Woven bamboo curtains were rolled up all around, to be let down for privacy or inclement weather. Belongings were stored in intricately carved and inlaid chests of Chinese workmanship. It was a treat to my eyes.

Leaving Pearl Harbor in the company of our sister ship, **U.S.S. Philadelphia** CL-41, five destroyers, and a fleet tanker, our little force crossed the Equator where we

---

[28] Pago Pago is pronounced Pango Pango; honest it is. Look it up in the dictionary. As the story goes (probably apocryphal) the 'n' was faulty on the typewriter the missionary used to describe this harbor town on the island of Tutuila.

'pollywogs' were initiated by old timer 'shell-backs,' and became shell-backs ourselves. An elaborate canvas swimming pool was erected on deck. On thrones and facing the pool sat King Neptune and his family. There was the Queen, the Princess royal, and the royal baby. Flowing tresses made of teased-out rope graced the heads of the two 'females', while the King wore elegant robes. The royal baby? He wore a diaper.

Each pollywog was assigned an outlandish uniform. Mine was an aviator's fur-lined flying suit and stockinged feet. From an old saying, "Women 'glow', men perspire, and horses sweat," I must be a horse; all my life I have been cursed with profuse sweating whenever hot. The pollywogs paraded around the entire ship, led *very slowly* by an unfortunate wearing a deep-sea diving suit complete with lead boots. Every step I took was marked with a footprint of sweat. (The aviators were upset at this use of their gear. The suit had to be turned inside out to dry before cleaning. They said it would never be the same.)

After suffering mild shocks from a huge battery powered aluminum electric knife wielded by the royal physician, I made my bows to the royal family and was seated in the 'judgment chair' mounted on the rim of the swimming pool. After I was convicted of treason to King Neptune, the hinged chair flipped me backward into the pool. In the pool were shell-backs armed with canvas clubs stuffed with kapok. While beating me with the clubs they tried to duck me to force me to say "shell-back." Having rather powerful legs, I refused to be ducked or say "shell-back." Dragging three or four shell-backs with me, I made it to the other side of the pool and out. Perhaps I am not a true shell-back, but I have my certificate card signed by Commander Denebrink which says I am. On the **Chicago**, the pollywogs mutinied, took over the ship, and flew the 'Jolly Roger', (skull and crossbones) from the mast!

Shortly after the crossing, the heavy cruiser **Chicago** CA-29 and another heavy cruiser, whose name I forgot, left us with their destroyers to go to Australia. After passing many intriguing atolls with their swaying and beckoning palms, we entered Pago Pago Harbor on the Samoan island of Tutuila.

The next day, our usual hiking group went ashore, carrying our water-filled canteens. We had spotted a pass in the mountains overlooking the town, and decided to go for it. After saying "No" to a man in town trying to 'rent' us a young girl, we proceeded toward the pass, following a well-used trail. Sensitive plants bordered the trail. It was funny to see the leaves fold up in disgust when my drops of sweat (of which I had plenty) fell on them. It was hot in the valley, and a group of schoolboys asked if we were thirsty. "Yes, yes!" we answered. One of them tied his ankles together with a length of rope, which helped him climb the smooth trunk of a coconut palm tree. He threw down several coconuts from up high. Borrowing our knives, the kids sharpened some stakes, and, with them, husked the coconuts. They broke a hole in each one, and handed them to us. The juice was cool and so refreshing! We tried to reward them, but they refused. We left some money in the trail anyway, and we were rewarded ourselves when they sang us some songs in sweet harmony.

The kids pointed out a zig-zag trail up to the pass and a shorter one which went straight up across the zig-zags. They let us know the zig-zag trail was for women and old men. The short-cut was for *men*, meaning themselves. (We took the zig-zags.)

The short trail down the other side led to a village where we were invited to join the group of men in each *fale*. Calling us 'Chief,' the occupants of each *fale* waved us in. Selecting one of the bigger ones, we entered and sat.

America Samoa had been governed by the U.S. Navy since it was received by division from Germany in 1900. Navy officers were seldom seen. As a result, Chief Petty Officers (CPOs) were the 'bosses' as far as Samoans knew. It was an honor to be called Chief. We found out in that *fale* that <u>all</u> Samoan men were 'chiefs.' There was one high chief, a few 'numbered chiefs,' and all the rest were 'talking chiefs.' These chiefs sat in their *fales* all day, talking, while the women did the work (fishing, gathering vegetables, etc.) Not a bad plan! For clothing, the Samoans wore what they called 'lava-lavas', popularized in the movies as 'sarongs,' (from a different part of the Pacific).

We were offered coconut cups full of a muddy-looking liquid dipped from a large wooden bowl. Having been warned on the ship not to drink water in Samoa, we refused, bringing gales of laughter when we pointed to our canteens in explanation. Later, Dr. Cross, the ship's dentist, an expert in these matters, told us we should have accepted. He explained, "*Kava*, as this drink is called, leaves you unaffected as long as you sit. It is only when you stand up that the effects, somewhat paralytic, are felt." When we learned how *kava* is prepared, we were glad we desisted. The village virgins sit around the bowl chewing starchy taro roots. When thoroughly chewed, each mouthful is spit into the bowl. Their saliva turns the starch into sugar which ferments, forming the beer called *kava*. Whee!

It was in this village I saw the wisdom of our order not to swim from the beaches. Three or four of the chiefs had 'elephantiasis', a disease caused by beach-dwelling nematode worms which invade the body through the soles. After years of exposure, one of the legs swells grotesquely until the foot looks like that of an elephant, circular in footprint, with toes spread on the circumference. Unsightly, but not deadly.

On the way back, we used the *men's* short-cut going down the other side. Again, it was hot, and, again, we were rescued from thirst. This time, an old man shinnied up the tree for our coconuts. He had a different idea about what we wanted, for our coconut drinks were fermented and fizzy! He had no qualms about accepting our tips. (He sang us no songs, either.)

That night, Padre Manion had arranged for entertainment on our after deck. (Arranging ship's entertainments was one of his jobs.) A troop of Samoan warriors performed several war and hunting dances to the accompaniment of drums and chanting. The hit of the evening was the sword dance the high chief's beautiful daughter did with a young fellow. It was quite dangerous. The swords were sharp blades mounted on long handles, in total about five feet long. They would swing these swords, barely missing each other. Sometimes she would lift her head just enough to have his blade come within an inch of her throat. She retaliated in kind. All she wore above the waist were a myriad of bead necklaces covering her bosom thoroughly, – *-until* – her father came up behind her and pulled all the necklaces up to her neck, baring her breasts! She kept her cool – she was too occupied to pull the necklaces down again – but you should have heard the delighted crew howl!

The next day, it was decided the crew should be allowed to swim, though not from the beaches. Instead, the ship's boats were put in the harbor, each with two Ensigns who took turns swimming while the other watched. Different Divisions took turns in the harbor water with different officers. I had fun swimming that day. Several days later, some of us didn't feel so good about it – myself, for instance. On the inside of one elbow I found what the 'sick bay' said was ringworm. A bunch of us contracted it from the harbor water. A liberal swabbing of salicylic acid (burned like Hell, it did!) took care of it, though even fifteen years later, the spot still showed up white when I got cold.

About this time, one of the new 90-day wonders, thinking I must know everything, being in the 'old Navy,' came to my cabin and asked me if I knew anything about syphilis. He said he was innocent of any encounter with a woman, but he had this sore in his crotch area. After he described the sore, I told him I thought he had ringworm. "Just go to the sick bay and tell them to put salicylic acid on it." A few minutes later I heard a mad running in the passage to my cabin. The poor fellow burst into the cabin, yelling, "Blow the fan on me, for God's sake!" in the meantime pulling down his pants. He was cured, I guess, but crotches have more pain nerves than elbows, and the corpsmen were quite liberal with their acid, I think.

Another victim of the harbor was the 'bull' (senior) Ensign Jaekel who got the ringworm in one ear so painfully he couldn't stand his engine-room watches for a while. Instead of a four-section watch, we were reduced to a three-section watch in the engine room. With watches, battle stations, quarters for muster and drills, changing from engine room dungarees to whites for meals, E-Division work, not to mention showers, shaving, etc., there was hardly time to sleep or eat until Jake recovered. Yes, I'll remember Samoa.

19

"You Are Steaming
Into Peril on the Sea!"

It was a straight shot over the sea from the delightful port of Pago Pago, in American Samoa, to Auckland, New Zealand. We passed beautiful verdant atolls of the South Pacific on our 'scenic' cruise. As we were under strict 'radio silence,' no response was made to the many imperative messages sent to **U.S.S. Brooklyn** (CL-40). Dispatch after dispatch came in stressing the importance of a reply, but orders are orders, and neither the Captain nor his 'Exec.' would *dream* of violating orders! Finally, a message was received from someone too exalted to disregard. Who the sender was, I don't know, but he used words so familiar to graduates of the Naval Academy that their authenticity was undoubted: "You are steaming into peril on the sea!" The *Sailors' Hymn*[29] is second only to *Anchors Aweigh* in the

---

[29] ***Eternal Father, Strong to Save*** (Sailors' Hymn). William Whiting & John Bacchus Dykes. 1861-1862: "...O hear us when we cry to Thee... For those in peril on the sea."

hearts of Academy graduates. The refrain in the hymn asks mercy 'For those *in peril on the sea.*' These powerful words convinced Captain Stone. **Brooklyn** broke the 'radio silence' to find us in a fearful situation.

A vast minefield had been laid off the shores of New Zealand, completely blocking all access to Auckland except for a narrow coastal corridor starting miles north of Auckland. We were steaming for the very center of the minefield, and were within a few miles! Washington had been trying its best to warn us. No way would we have escaped! De-gaussing equipment was useless here; these were conventional mines, exploding on contact.

Once communication was established, it was arranged for a New Zealand Pilot to meet us at the entrance to the secure corridor to guide us into Auckland harbor and safety. No wonder Washington was so desperate to get our response. I wonder who it was who finally sent that convincing message. Could it have been the President, who always had a liking for the **Brooklyn**?

The Pilot met us and we went steaming grandly along the New Zealand coast. I was on the bridge, wearing a 'sound powered' headset to direct the settings of the de-gaussing switches down in the forward engine room. I could hear the Pilot conversing with Captain Stone, pointing out landmarks along the shore. We were close in to land. As we passed a wrecked freighter lying on the bottom, the Pilot casually remarked that the ship had been sunk only two days ago by a magnetic mine, that 'egg' probably laid by a Japanese submarine to be 'hatched' by the unfortunate freighter. **Then** - - -

"Mr. Cragg! Mr. Cragg! We just lost power on the switchboard!" - - - What to do? It would take a mile or more to stop a ship the size of the **Brooklyn**. But I had confidence in my man and knew he could have the power restored pronto. I told him to get it back *right now*! In less than a minute power was restored. If we had encountered a magnetic mine in that minute, we would have been hit no matter what action I had just taken. I acted wisely. What turmoil had I blown the whistle! There would have been courts-martial all over the place, especially including me since the Electrician's Mate was in my division. The *real* culprit would have gone innocently on his way, though I would have fought to include him. Not much chance of that since he wore the Naval Academy 'fraternity ring', and what was I?

In October, 1940, when the de-gaussing coils were installed in the **Brooklyn**, I requested installing a protective grating to shield the exposed high voltage connections at the back of the de-gaussing switchboard. Mr. Herring, the Lieutenant Commander who OK'd ship's expenditures in his capacity as the **Brooklyn**'s 'First Lieutenant,' was out to make a name for himself. First Lieutenants who saved money were given good 'annual fitness reports,' essential to peacetime promotion. My request was turned down, as described in Chapter 7.

Next to the de-gaussing switchboard was a desk, and on this desk was a huge home-made coffee mug soldered from heavy copper. Things 'jiggle' when a ship is underway, and the desk was no exception. Jiggled to the side and out into the open 'bus bars', the copper mug plunged, coffee and all. The resulting 'fireworks' were described to me later by the men. I cautioned them to *keep their 'traps' shut!* These were 'good' fireworks. Because of them, the men knew where to look and how to fix the problem.

By the next morning, and without my knowledge, a protective grating had been fabricated and installed around the switchboard! How strange! Where the grating came from or how it got there I do not know; but I knew better than to ask. Mr. Herring, the real villain of this 'adventure,' never heard about this 'unauthorized use' of material. When in charge of good men, it is better, when turned down, to just wish out loud near the crew how much you would have liked whatever it was. Miracles happen when men have been treated squarely.

Other instances occurred when Mr. Herring was by-passed, all funny, but they were less important, not 'life or death.' Maybe I'll get around to them. Oh well, here's one of them. I was the 'movie officer' who selected the movies to be shown on the 'fantail' (after-deck) and two of my Electrician's Mates got the films from the flagship and ran them through the projectors. The machines were somewhat worn, and their 'French Gray' instrument enamel needed a bit of touching up. I requested enough enamel to do the job, but was told to use gray 'war color' paint at one-tenth the cost. The next time I saw the machines, they were all spruced up in 'French Gray' instrument enamel. I knew better than to ask questions. Was the ship bankrupt for using a pint of expensive enamel? Probably not – for the cost was partially offset by not using a pint of war color.

20
The Date That Never Was:
A Poignant Little Episode

There were two such dates, a Friday in March when the **U.S.S. Brooklyn** crossed the International Date Line, and the other, a date with an unknown girl in New Zealand. Friday, March 14th, 1941, never existed for the ship or its crew; the date just never was. We skipped from Thursday the 13th to Saturday the 15th but made up for it on our return trip with a double day.[30] The other date that never was? It would have been so idyllic had it happened!

What to do this first day in New Zealand? I know - I'll walk around and select my murder victims – as everyone I met in New Zealand expected when they heard I was from Chicago. At first, I thought they were kidding. They weren't! – What I discovered instead was a group of beautiful Gothic buildings of carved gray limestone. As I gazed at the buildings, a distinguished looking gentleman came up to me and, in his upper-class British accent, asked if he could be of assistance. When told the Gothic architecture of these

---

[30]Coming back, we had two Saturdays back to back. It was puzzling how to begin the engine room log for the mid-watch (midnight), but I finally wrote "Saturday Number 2." How it was done in the ship's log on the bridge, I don't know (or really care).

buildings reminded me so much of the University of Chicago, he was excited. "This is the University of New Auckland, and I am Professor of Architecture. Would you like a tour of the campus?" "Certainly," was my reply. "Unfortunately," he said, "I must go to a meeting but would you mind if my clerk took you around?" Well! That clerk was gorgeous Barbara Allen with shiny dark hair, sparkling eyes, and a figure to match! Her name brought me thoughts of my lost love, Barbara Washburn. We had parted sadly for the last time a year ago.

The tour was great! Barbara took me into classrooms where she introduced me to students who, in turn, stared at what was probably the first American Navy uniform they had ever seen. The last U.S. Navy visit had been in 1925.

Among the students was a chap with an unusual tale. He was a 'parolee.' His ship had been sunk by a German raider.[31] After adding him to the prisoners already on board the raider, the Germans marooned them on a remote island. after all signed 'paroles' that they would not take up arms against Germany. If one of them did and was taken prisoner, he would be automatically executed according to the 'Rules of War.' Being excused from military service, this able-bodied young man was on campus instead of being in uniform. I found his story most interesting.

We got along well, Barbara and I, so we made a date to meet at her office after work. We would dine somewhere and take in a show. What a beautiful evening to look forward to!

Returning to the ship to freshen up for my date was a sad error. If only I had been satisfied with the way I was.

---

[31]The presence of German raiders and Japanese submarines in the South Pacific in 1941 was the reason the ships in our little force flew their largest American flags all night (contrary to flag etiquette). The flags were brightly lit by searchlights too. It's not pleasant to be torpedoed, even by mistake.

Entering the Wardroom (officers' hangout), I was greeted with "Oh, good! Here's another one. Mister Cragg, you are to be a guest at the Army barracks thirty miles out of town." "But–but I can't! I have a date!" "Oh, no you don't! There aren't enough officers to go around to all the affairs arranged for us. You are *ordered* to go! The bus leaves in thirty minutes." There was no way to let poor Barbara know about this, so she was stood up. To this day, it gives me a bad feeling to picture her waiting patiently at her desk for Ensign Cragg who never arrived. I wrote her a letter of explanation and apology, to which she replied that she had guessed what had happened and it was OK.

The Army camp? That requires another chapter (or perhaps two).

P.S. I have since learned that the Professor of Architecture at University of Auckland in 1941 was Professor Cyril Roy Knight. (From the kind research by Wendy Garvey, Architecture Librarian at the University of Auckland.)

21
Guests of the New Zealand Army

Have you ever heard a *Haka*? Not very likely, but I have, a thousand of them at once! A sound never to forget; a sound so alarming that it startled even us, the potential allies of these New Zealand people.

What is a *haka*? Each Maori warrior, from childhood, has practiced it – his own personal war cry, complete with horrible facial gestures. The tongue is extended as far downward as possible. After a lifetime, it is amazing how close to the chin some tongues can get. All-in-all, a frightening combination (as intended).

Here we were, in a very large building, all under one roof, filled with shrieking Maori warriors. I should have been with beautiful Barbara Allen on our way to some nice quiet restaurant in Auckland, 30 miles away. As soon as our bus arrived at the army camp, we were herded into this huge hall to see the Maori troops and for them to see us. Our entrance was the inspiration for the *hakas*, helped by the beer bar extending the full length of the building. If you think a rock concert with full amplification is loud, *it is a whisper compared to what assaulted our ears that night!*

Each Maori wanted to shake our hands, and each Maori showed his manliness by how hard he could squeeze.

After two or three, I caught on and grabbed first. Even so, my hand swelled to half again its normal size, and was painful for days afterward.

These guys were not kidding about their toughness. They were later sent to North Africa, where they fought Rommel's Germans. Soon, the Germans did everything they could not to be stationed opposite these Maoris. Tales seeped out of the Sahara about what happened there. Maoris take no prisoners! It was rumored that what soldiers were captured were executed after being forced to eat their own testicles (suitably prepared, of course). After all, these Maoris were only one or two generations removed from cannibals (Barbara Allen letter to me in America, 3/4/42), and rumor had it that 'long pig' might still be eaten in remote regions of New Zealand. I'm glad we had beef in the officers' mess that night. Human tastes like pork, it is said[32], and this was *not* pork.

After the ordeal of Maori exuberance, we were quietly escorted to cocktails and dinner in the officers' mess. The officers were all of English descent – no Maoris – and spoke in the upper class British accent which seemed to be the norm in New Zealand. (They did not sound like Australian 'Crocodile Dundee'.) A young officer appointed himself my dinner companion and sat next to me. How much nicer it would have been with Barbara Allen anywhere else!

---

[32] *20,000 Leagues Over the Sea.* William R. Robinson. Robinson sailed the 32 foot ketch **Svaap** around the world in the 1930s. His cannibalism took place in New Guinea. He thought the meat was pork until he was told, after the meal, it was 'long pig' from a tribe up the river. He later married a Dodge heiress. When he and his bride tried to repeat the voyage in a much larger boat, he got appendicitis in the Galapagos Islands. His bride's family had considerable influence. A U.S. destroyer, complete with doctor, was sent to his rescue.

Soon the toasts were flowing, the officers using every conceivable excuse to toss one down. We started with Roosevelt: 'Hear-hear!" Then came King George: "Hear-hear!" Then came the U.S. Navy, and then the New Zealand Army. On and on it went. I lifted my glass each time, but only to take the least taste. After a while my young companion quietly asked in a slurred voice, "Would you help me go outdoors? I don't feel well at all." With my assistance (he did not walk steadily) we reached the open air. He mumbled, "I don't know what happened. We knew you had 'dry' ships, and we were going to drink all of you under the tables. You were my 'assignment', but here I am, being helped out by you. I think I am drunk. Oh, my parents would be so ashamed! How do you do it?" I nonchalantly replied, "Oh, we know how to handle these things."

In the meantime, on board the **Brooklyn**, several young ladies had been invited to dinner. Had I been one of the watch-standers, those unfortunate ones who must remain on board, Barbara Allen could have been my guest that night. While all were waiting for Commander Denebrink to enter before they could be seated, a sweet young thing asked if they were to have drinks before dinner. When it was explained that we had no liquor in our ships, she burst out in a piercing voice, "Good Heavens! How do you keep your peckers up?" Her escort turned bright red, and not a word was spoken for a while. A friend of mine, on returning from England, showed me a photograph of a sign saying, *"Drink Bovril – Keep Your Pecker Up!"* It would not have bothered me had I heard Barbara Allen say these words. There is a language difference, and what is meant is one's spirit.

After my friend finished his vomiting, and we returned to the mess hall, the toasts had been concluded. The poor 'Leftenant' (another Britishism) managed the meal portion of the evening as best as he could.

A bit more about language difficulties – a couple of E Division men got into mild trouble when they asked for a napkin instead of a serviette. The waitress thought they needed a diaper. I, in turn, asked for some adhesive tape in a chemist's shop (drugstore.) "Adhesive tape – what is that?" "That's what that is," I replied, pointing to some in the counter. "Oh, you mean sticking plahstuh [plaster]." The funny thing is that when she got it out, it said, "Adhesive Tape – Made by Johnson & Johnson, U.S.A." "Oh, I never noticed that before." Some customs can be life-threatening. Looking to the left, and seeing no cars coming, I stepped off the curb to be almost run over by a tiny car which was being driven on the left side of the street. What a strange way to die so far from home.

Now a final word about Maori warriors, their officers, college Professors, and opinions about Chicago. The good name of my city had been eroded worldwide by movies such as *Little Caesar*[33]. Carl Sandburg did nothing to mitigate Chicago's reputation either when he penned these words about the city, "...And they tell me you are crooked and I answer: Yes, it is true I have seen the gunman kill and go free to kill again..."[34].

Reaction to my Chicago origin seemed to be on three levels in New Zealand. There was that of the Maori warrior. The Army officer had a more knowledgeable bias. The opinion of a university Professor was well removed from either of these categories.

The Maori warrior, had he heard of Chicago's tough reputation, would have shrugged it off. In his mind, *he* is the epitome of toughness! "Listen to me as I strike fear into everyone with my *haka* war-cry and my fierce grimace. See

---

[33]Starring Edgar G. Robinson. Warner Brothers. Directed by Mervyn LeRoy. (1931).
[34]*Chicago.* Carl Sandburg, Poetry Magazine (1914).

how I grip the hands of these Americans so strongly that they wince."

New Zealand Army officers were of a different stripe. They had indeed heard of Chicago, and were not joking when they revealed their misgivings about it. Said I, "I was born and raised in Chicago, and I never saw anyone murdered." My disavowal did nothing to dispel nervousness about me in the minds of New Zealand Army officers in 1941. After two or three of these encounters, I just said I came from Illinois.

The distinguished Professor of Architecture at the University of Auckland was frank in his admiration of cultural Chicago. He knew of our magnificent Art Institute and our breathtaking lakefront. Of course he was familiar with the 'Prairie School' of architecture and its Frank Lloyd Wright. When I mentioned the University of Chicago with its Gothic buildings of Indiana limestone, he even knew that subject too. Gangsters? If he had heard of them, they were evidently unimportant to him.

In conclusion, it is fine for me to be proud of Chicago, but there have been times when it was more comfortable to refrain from 'Chicagoism'[35]. To the Maori warrior, the bragging would have been meaningless. To his officer, it would have been intimidating. Only to the well-educated person would there have been meaning, but it would have been in poor taste to boast to such a listener.

---

[35] Manatee Community College Professor, Blake Wiley, points out to his class that any subject can be reduced to an 'ism' resulting in a proliferation of 'isms' in modern usage. His final exam. asked for the expounding of an 'ism', any 'ism'. If one isn't available, create one. This section is extracted from a final exam. paper of mine titled 'Chicagoism'.

22
Rotorua

On our second day in New Zealand, our group was scheduled for a trip to Rotorua, New Zealand's 'Yellowstone Park.' This was an all day trip. No chance to see Barbara Allen or even call her to explain! This was our next to last day here before we depart, and already we were scheduled for tomorrow's boring parties and dinners with no escape possible. A watch was perhaps kept on me to make sure I didn't try to evade some of this relentless hospitality.

The train to Rotorua was a special for us with tracks cleared for the 130 mile trip at speeds of over 100 miles per hour – so said the train-men. The first fifteen cars were for enlisted personnel, followed by the officers' car, and last, but not least, a baggage car filled with all kinds of alcoholic beverages. After some original hesitancy, the crew members began a steady stream back and forth through our car to the booze. Some of the officers also visited the baggage car, notably the dentist, Dr. L.L. Cross and the Chief Warrant Gunner, Mr. Hydinger.

Our train passed through mile after mile of strange looking tall plants, as big as trees, yet not trees. Someone in the car knew they were 'tree ferns', not seen anywhere else in the world except in conservatory greenhouses, it was said.

There were also many flocks of sheep, grazing on a wide plain with a beautiful mountain background.

At the Rotorua station, limousines were lined up to take the officers to a reception and banquet. Dr. Cross and Mr. Hydinger espied a pretty half-caste Maori girl standing on the platform with a little boy. "Is that yours?" Dr. Cross asked her, indicating the little boy. She shook her head "No." "How'd you like to have a doctor?" was the next thing I heard the dentist say. Much to the consternation of the waiting Rotorua officials, Dr. Cross and Mr. Hydinger proceeded to load her into one of the limousines. On arrival at the hotel, the officials (and the rest of us) breathed a sigh of relief when the dentist and the Gunner walked down the street with the girl instead of bringing her into the hotel.

After the dinner, followed by the usual speeches, we had a tour of the thermal grounds. Spouting pools of various colors, hot mud pots, and boiling springs reminded me of the sights I saw in Yellowstone while traveling through on a motorcycle in the summer of 1937[36]. The thermal grounds formed a fitting backdrop for Maori war dances complete with hakas and fierce faces, followed by more peaceful dances by the 'wahines' (women) swinging little balls on strings (poi balls) in time to the music of their harmonic singing. Captain Stone was greeted by the elder lady of the Maoris, Rangi, who rubbed noses with him. He resented with a glaring scowl the laughter this caused.

The hot swimming pool was a strange experience. After getting used to the reek of ancient rotten eggs, we got in the shallow, cooler end of the pool. Hot springs fed the

---

[36] I had ridden a Harley ' 74 ' from Indiana to Oregon to visit lovely Barbara Washburn whom I hadn't seen since she was five. We had corresponded for two years after I saw her picture on her Aunt's piano. This visit became five weeks. After another visit over the Christmas holidays, we were engaged !

deep end of the pool with un-softened, very hot sulfur water. Gradually getting acclimated, we went deeper until we became as hot as we individually wanted. We compared notes later and found that those who had used this pool had no dandruff (a ship-board occupational hazard) for several months after.

The day was over. Darkness and rain had descended, and it was time to board the train. Much to our relief, Dr. Cross and Mr. Hydinger showed up on time. One kissed the Maori girl goodbye on one cheek, while the other followed suit on the other side. They boarded the train with steady step, seemingly unaffected by the events of the day.

'Twas a dark and stormy night' as we rushed through the pitch black and rainy New Zealand countryside heading for Auckland and our ships after visiting fascinating Rotorua. With tracks cleared ahead of us, the special train was again traveling at high speed. Dr. Cross, the dentist and *kava* expert, became restless. Finally he went to the baggage car and returned with his jacket pockets full of bottles, stating, "I'm going forward where the men are, not just a bunch of 'poops' like you."

A little later, perhaps fifteen minutes or so, a Marine enlisted man poked his head in the door and asked, "Could some officer come forward and help us with Dr. Cross? He is giving us trouble, and enlisted men are not allowed to lay hands on an officer." My cabin-mate Bob Woodall – good ol' Woody – volunteered for the job. In a few minutes, the train began to slow down and finally came to a full stop. When Woody returned with Dr. Cross, he had a harrowing tale to tell. Dr. Cross had climbed a ladder between cars and was standing on the roof, bravely facing the wind and the rain. Woody got hold of a train crew member, explained the situation, and the train was brought to its gradual stop. Dr. Cross was indignant: "You *know* I like to go up on the bridge in a storm!"

The next morning, while I was eating breakfast in the Wardroom, Dr. Cross came in, wearing his bathrobe. His face was all nicked with razor cuts. "What happened yesterday?" he asked. When I told him, he groaned, "Omigod! All I can remember is getting about half-way to Rotorua."

This being our last day in New Zealand, we were still scheduled to more affairs than there were officers. I don't remember the day's affairs, but I do remember the food was better. Some cook got hold of some lamb before it turned into mutton, so it was tender and tasty. Along that line, the New Zealand Freezing Association gave the **Brooklyn** several tons of frozen sheep carcasses. At sea, we ate mutton chops 'til the lanolin was oozing out our pores. The rest was thrown overboard. Americans just aren't used to mutton.

23
Justice?

The ships of our little force were under 'radio silence' during our cruise to the South Pacific. What this meant was 'no communication of any kind from us to the rest of the world.' This included personal letters. We were ordered not to divulge our location to friends or family. However, President Roosevelt, in one of his 'fireside chats' on the radio after our arrival, not only told the world our ships had arrived on a good will mission to Australia and New Zealand, he even named the **Brooklyn** and the **Philadelphia,** as well as each of the five destroyers with us. One would think it safe to write the family about our whereabouts. At least one of us thought so, a Naval Academy graduate, Ensign Breed. The postal authorities in Auckland randomly pulled letters from our mailings. Mr. Breed's letter was opened. Mr. Breed had disobeyed a direct order; he had written to tell his mother where we were.

Mr. Breed was given a 'general court martial.' The trial lasted days. I looked in occasionally and saw the senior officers sitting in judgment on the trial. Ensign Breed was found guilty and sentenced to the loss of 100 numbers. For explanation, each class at the Academy is numbered by scholastic standing, starting with the bottom of the preceding class. In peacetime in 1941, the loss of 100 numbers spelled the end of his career to a naval officer – unless a transfer to Naval Aviation can be arranged. Ensign Breed must have had some 'clout', for he got his transfer, only to be killed in flight training at Pensacola. Those members of the court martial should have had terrible feelings of remorse about this, because most of them were probably equally guilty, but were not caught.

I was not guilty; I wrote no letters. Instead of a letter, I bought the Auckland newspapers telling about our visit, complete with pictures of the ships, descriptions of the ships, numbers in the crews of the ships, where we had been, on and on. These newspapers are still in my possession, saved by my mother for me after she received them by mail from New Zealand.

24
Tahiti

"What the Hell is that?" was our question as **U.S.S. Brooklyn** steamed through the channel between Moorea and Tahiti. "That" was a large wooden boat slowly overtaking us – but this boat had wings and was in the air! A very large biplane, whose fuselage was a real and heavy-appearing wooden boat, was approaching us from astern, just barely faster than our 18 knots. Standing on the flying boat's lower wings were a number of scantily-clad people holding onto the vertical struts between the wings. As we were waved to by the 'strap-hangers', this antique contraption passed slowly alongside, no higher than the main deck, and finally disappeared behind a headland several miles ahead. This was our introduction to Tahiti and Tahitians. I have often thought that, as the boat was near the water when landing in the lagoon, the temptation for the water-loving Tahitian wing-standers to dive in would be irresistible. I also wonder if those people were charged a fee for this sight-seeing 'tour' of the U.S. Navy ships.

While we were passing the island of Moorea, its fantastically distorted topography seemed like a vision from Dante's 'Divine Comedy'. The sky-scraping cores of mighty volcanos had solidified in grotesque and 'impossible' angles, revealed after the surrounding earth had washed away.

Then, as we approached the harbor of Tahiti, the strong smell of soap filled the air. Due to the War, ships had not come to Tahiti for months, and the copra (coconut meat used to make soap) stored on the Lever Brothers' wharf was spoiling. The spectacular view was not hurt by the odor, which was not all that bad. Past the reef which surrounded Tahiti, and behind the town of Papeete, rose high and verdant mountains; which our Hawaii-trained eyes recognized as ancient volcanos.

A Tahitian pilot came aboard to guide the ship through the reef and to its dock. The dock was for cruise ships, and had been unused far too long for the Tahitian economy. Captain Stone was fluent in French, so no interpreter was required for the pilot. Not all Naval Academy graduates were as linguistically versatile. Later, I acquired a following of Academy graduates, for I knew enough High School French to say "Combien?" [how much?] and "Trop cher!" [too dear] for those who wanted to deal with the Chinese merchants, who are known as the 'shop keepers of the Pacific'. (They were seen in Pago Pago too and were said to be on all islands of any size.)

Coming from a great time in New Zealand, we thought Tahiti was the frosting on the cake of our exciting voyage. As the first visitors for many a month, our ships were most welcome in Tahiti. The powers-that-be in Washington must really want to make us happy, we presumed. Papeete became crowded with people from all over the island coming to greet us and see us. I remember in particular a beautiful blonde in a riding outfit who rode a motorcycle from one end of Papeete to the other through the crowded street – back and forth – I never could figure that out. The crew and officers soon found Quinn's Bar, the main gathering place in Papeete. Shaped in a square U, it had booths with curtains which could be drawn closed. All sorts of food and drinks were served in Quinn's. Woody tried out Quinn's; I did not.

All those getting shore leave were ordered to get their dollars exchanged for francs at the bank. We soon found out we could get a much better deal from the Chinese merchants by illegally purchasing our South Pacific curios directly with dollars. The dollars would magically vanish under the counter, and our change would be copiously returned in francs, many more than the official exchange rate. At this late date, a court martial is doubtful, so I'm confessing now. A large piece of 'tapa' cloth from Tahiti adorned a wall in our cottage in Lakeside, Michigan, for years before finally disintegrating, and a Samoan sleeping mat of woven palm fronds was a floor runner upstairs – both bought in Tahiti with illegal dollars.

Some of the hiking group decided to climb the mountain behind Papeete. Following a path along a rushing stream, we began our ascent. Along the way, we came across a small roofless hut with water pouring down out of a pipe from upstream. Hearing feminine giggles, we were by-passing the hut when the door opened. Inside were two young Tahitian girls taking a shower. We were tempted to accept their invitation to join them, but we remembered a somber warning printed in the ship's bulletin and kept going.

Tahiti was not entirely the paradise it looked to be, we were informed. Facts about each port of call were circulated to all hands by bulletin. We learned the main industries of Tahiti were tourism and copra, both of which were zero since World War II began so many months ago on September 1, 1939. Cruise ships and freighters stopped coming; and Tahiti was in a deep economic depression. Also, the venereal disease rate in Tahiti exceeded 90%. We just said, "Bonjour" to the girls and left. They laughed.

We never did get to the top of the mountain. It became hot above the tree line, and the trail seemed to go on indefinitely. The mountain top stayed just as far off as when we started. I wanted to keep going, but was told I'd have to go it alone – the rest were turning around. So back to Papeete they went, and I went with them.

"At first I hated it with all my heart and soul, but I finally got used to it," she said. Woody was listening to the woes of the wife of an American couple at a booth in Quinn's. They had been living in Tahiti for several years, and one custom was still distasteful to the wife. Shortly after they took up residence, a pretty Tahitian girl walked into their house. She said, "I've come to take care of your husband." Assuming she was the cleaner, the wife tried, in her rudimentary French, to discuss what needed to be cleaned. "No, no. I am here to take your husband to bed. You go do shopping." Eventually this became the arrangement, but not that first time. Woody could hardly wait to tell me about it. I had thought about going in to Quinn's, but when I looked in and saw two pairs of feet, one pair bare and the other with Navy shoes, protruding through the curtains of one of the booths, I changed my mind about eating at any of those tables. Quinn's was demolished in the 1970s due to too many riots and 'unspeakable acts' on premises.

Tahiti had a bad effect on some of the crew. A young Marine hanged himself under a ladder below decks. He was cut down in time, much to the disgust of Dr. Manlove, who told us, "They should have let him finish the job." The doctor also said a number of venereal cases had showed up in spite of the warning in the ship's bulletin. (No officers, though.)

Though it was exquisitely beautiful, I was just as glad to see the last of Tahiti. Perhaps the arrival of two cruisers and five destroyers, after many months with no visitors, was overwhelming. Others who have been there in peacetime have had a different impression from mine, and I am being prudish and unfair, I suppose.

Woody and I were soon to learn the real reason we stopped in Tahiti on our way back to Hawaii from New Zealand. It was not for pleasure.

25
Revolution in Paradise

"Come on, Woody." I said to my cabin-mate, "Let's go to Honolulu harbor and see that sixty-five foot schooner **Chance** just in from Tahiti." The *Honolulu Advertiser* that morning told about three couples who subsisted on nothing but potatoes the last week of their voyage from Tahiti to Hawaii. Sailing craft are interesting, and we had just returned from Tahiti ourselves. (We could have run them down at night!) Ensign Woodall agreed, so we donned our civilian clothes, and left our light cruiser 'home', **U.S.S. Brooklyn**.

"Dick Cragg! What the Hell are *you* doing here?" These words emanated from a head protruding from the hatchway of the good-looking schooner **Chance**. The rest of my unexpected and lengthy schoolmate from high-school, Chris Sergel (pole-vaulter on the track team that I had captained), emerged from the hatch, and we told each other our respective adventures. Chris, his wife Faith, and two other University of Chicago graduate couples bought the **Chance** after six Harvard graduates sailed it around the world. With the supreme confidence typical of U. of C. graduates (Purdue was *my* 'alma mater') they hired an 'old salt' to teach them the arcane arts of sailing and navigation while sailing from New York to Bermuda. From Bermuda, without their mentor, the six adventurers sailed to the Galapagos Islands via the Panama Canal, and on to Tahiti, where they soon made themselves at home.

The French paradise of Tahiti harbored a lurking 'serpent' personified by local officials controlled from the 'Vichy' government in France (under Hitler's dictates). Though the United States was not yet at war, Chris and his crew took part in the Tahitian portion of the struggle between the 'viper' of Vichy and the 'Free French' government led from London by General Charles de Gaulle. Our friends helped the Free French of Tahiti overthrow the Vichy government of that lovely and troubled spot! (Not very 'neutral' were our people, were they? – but hooray for our side!) Following the revolution, their schooner **Chance** was even used to transport the Vichy officials to exile on a nice isolated island.

From Chris and Faith we learned why our ships had visited beautiful Tahiti. The United States consul to Tahiti had sided with the 'Vichy' officials against the 'Free French' and was now *persona non grata* in Tahiti. Our ships were ordered there to take our consul away – far away! He was taken back to Hawaii in the other cruiser of our force, **U.S.S. Philadelphia**. Even the wildest 'scuttlebutt' rumors had left us ignorant until now. Wait 'til we two 'big mouths' get back to the **Brooklyn**!

Chris Sergel then told us about his new trouble. The other two couples in the crew found they liked Hawaii [who doesn't?] and 'jumped ship' (quit). He needed a crew to sail the **Chance** back to the mainland, but it was not easy to get a crew in Hawaii. [If only I weren't in the Navy!------------------ Oh well.]

26
Whiplash

How should one sail from Hawaii to California? Go east? No, not if the vessel is sail-powered. Going east meant beating against the trade wind blowing from the American continent, a laborious, tiring procedure, and slow. Those who sail know that the fastest and most comfortable way to sail is with the wind a-beam or on a broad reach. When going north from Hawaii, the trade wind affords such a luxury. To the north, just south of the Aleutian Islands, there usually exists a weather phenomenon known as the 'Aleutian high' – an area of high barometric pressure from which winds blow radially outward all around. The sailor going north from Hawaii on his beam trade wind will find another beam wind blowing west as he reaches the area of the 'high'. Keeping the wind always a-beam, he will automatically circle around the high to its north, rounding eventually to the east, then south-east ending up just off the west coast of Alaska, still on a beam wind. He has been catapulted around the high as a skater is flung off the end of the line in the 'crack the whip' or 'whiplash' stunt. In many ways, the technique is akin to the way NASA uses the larger planets to sling their space explorers off in the desired direction.

Going south along the Alaskan coast, the outward wind from the high is joined by prevailing westerly winds found on this coast, so he still has his nice beam wind as he heads south towards California. South of Yakutat, Alaska, our sailor has the option of either taking the protected 'Inside Passage' past Sitka and Ketchikan, or remaining at sea in the Pacific with its dangerous storms. Chris Sergel took the whiplash to Alaska and the States.

Chris found his crew for **Chance** and made a profit as well. The *Honolulu Advertiser* had written about his effort to find a crew, and soon he had applicants galore. When they actually offered to *pay* for a chance to sail on this 'romantic' voyage, he had no trouble picking a combination of the highest fares and the highest competence. There was one who went free: a mechanic who fixed the engine and would keep it in good shape. There was one other who was not competent, but merely ornamental: a Honolulu socialite who offered the highest fare of all. It was like finding the 'golden fleece' for Chris's 'Argosy' with these unexpected fares. He bought plenty of provisions beside potatoes this time.

On the day the **Chance** sailed, Woody, the Husseys, and I went to the Honolulu harbor mouth to see them go. There was a big crowd, attracted by the newspaper articles, but Chris and Faith spotted us as they putt-putted by and returned our waves with vigor. As for the socialite, she was due for a rude awakening once **Chance** emerged into the great Pacific rollers. As the boat went by us, she was standing on deck "with a stay in one hand and a far away look in the other," as I wrote my mother at the time. She was certainly lovely and dressed in the most stylish sea-going togs, but standing around on a sailboat is neither comfortable nor safe. Standing only when it is required is the usual way to behave. She probably soon learned who was Captain of that little ship. We watched until they were out of sight. Little did we know that the **Brooklyn** would reach the mainland before the **Chance**.

27
Scuttlebutt

A *scuttlebutt* is a barrel or keg with a spigot or tap. *Butt* is Middle English for a barrel or keg and *scuttle* is Middle English for a hole, speaking nautically (*The American Heritage Dictionary*). The scuttlebutt was used on old sailing ships to provide drinking water. It was natural for two or more crew members to meet at the scuttlebutt to exchange gossip and rumors. This practice evolved to where 'scuttlebutt' meant rumor spreading and gossip. (This is also practiced at office water coolers.) Water coolers aboard warships are still called scuttlebutts, though they are now modern drinking fountains, welded to the deck to prevent them from being missiles in case of a hit, or even a near miss. This lesson was learned from British experience early in World War II. The nice porthole in Woody's and my cabin was lost to us for the same reason – that it could become a missile. A steel plate was welded over it by men from the fleet tender **Antares** when we reached Pearl Harbor. We really missed that porthole because our hot cabin was over one of the 'fire rooms' (boilers). Though we had a fan, many were the times I couldn't decide, while lying in my bunk, if it was a drop of sweat or a cockroach running down my side. Pajamas had been put away after I came aboard because taking them off before putting on clothes added to the time it took to reach my battle station in the after engine room. All water tight doors and hatches are dogged down five minutes after general quarters is sounded. After that, permission from the Captain is required to open each of these if a person is late. Incidentally, those small 'oriental' cockroaches bite!

We were on maneuvers in early May, practicing for the time when it might become real for us. All eight boilers had steam so we could execute 'flank speed' (maximum) on demand. We were to return to Pearl Harbor that weekend. The Husseys were expecting Woody and me for a luau in honor of my birthday, May 8th. One day, a destroyer came alongside and, with a line-throwing gun, shot a line across our fore-deck. A message was hauled over in a sealed container for 'Captain's eyes only.' All of us engine room watch-standers were called into the Chief Engineer, Lieutenant Commander Cavenagh's office. We were told to immediately shut down all boilers but the three we used for economical cruising. Our speed was reduced to our usual eighteen knots for saving fuel, and economy was stressed.

It was at this time in Mr. Cavenagh's office that we, who stood watch in the engine room, realized that our Chief Engineer knew less engineering than we did! He told us to steam under a slightly darker brown haze "to save oil." "I Dream of Steaming With a Light Brown Haze," sung to the tune of 'Jeannie', is the song of the black gang. Light brown haze from our stack results from a slightly inefficient mixture of fuel with air using a 'tad' more oil than perfect. Slightly more air gives a clear stack and best efficiency, but is hard to monitor. Even more air *still* gives a clear stack, looking the same but burning less efficiently – wasting oil. A *lot* more air results in ugly yellow-white smoke and terrible efficiency. Therefore, to get almost perfect efficiency, we use the 'light brown haze' rule which is easy to follow. Mr. Cavenagh, suggesting a darker haze, was asking for a waste of oil, and showing us all that he didn't know what he was talking about. We didn't dare look at each other, we might have laughed, but we all knew to continue 'steaming with a light brown haze' like we always did.

In the meantime, the ship's course had been changed to southeast, which was directly opposite to Hawaii, much to the distress of the majority of the crew who had families in the Islands. Where to?

'Scuttlebutt' flourished beyond reason. "We're going to the Galapagos Islands," or, "We're searching for Count Von Luckner," the famous German raider from World War I who was rumored to Captain a raider in the Pacific[37]. You name it; we had the rumor. When the name **Brooklyn** was removed from the ship by men suspended over the stern, and our number, CL-40, was painted over by men suspended on each side of the bow, the rumors became wilder. They were really wild when even the '**Bro**' letters were pried off all the ship's boats. What the heck is happening to us?

When we reached the Equator, our course was changed to due east. Wow, was it hot on that Equator! The forward engine room became especially hot when its main exhaust blower burned out. Having hardly any ventilation caused a Hellish atmosphere. Our 'ship riggers' hoisted the huge electric motor up several decks to our shop. (My division was the E, or electrical, division of thirty-five men.) We had the replacements for the burned-out coils, and my men soon had them installed, but there were no instructions for connecting them. If done wrong, the motor could run at double speed, half speed, or in reverse at half, correct, or double speed. Going back in my memory to my 1936 AC Machinery course at Purdue University, I had to re-design the motor from scratch to obtain the correct direction and speed. Although I appeared confident, my nerves were on edge

---

[37] This was an obvious mistake on the part of the rumor starter. Luckner was strongly anti-Nazi and was almost imprisoned. Only his fame and popularity saved him from jail or worse.

when the motor was installed and turned on. It worked perfectly! After that, Ensign Cragg was no longer just a Reserve officer figurehead to my men. It was "Mr. Cragg, what about this?" and "Mr. Cragg, what about that?" The young 'strikers' (working towards promotion) were asking me to tutor them in Math and Electricity. It felt good.

About this time, President Roosevelt declared that what had been a 'limited emergency' was now an 'unlimited emergency.' My year of active duty to change my commission from probationary to permanent would be over in September, but Mr. Cavenagh assured me that now there was no possibility of my returning to inactive status.

More fuel to the scuttlebutt factory occurred when the **Brooklyn** turned abruptly northeast, directly toward the Panama Canal. Now what?

Of all things, our transit through the Canal was at night! If spies, with which Panama was loaded, were expected not to notice that a **Brooklyn** class light cruiser, with its distinctive five turrets with three six-inch guns each, was going through, somebody did not 'have the picture.' Not only was it a **Brooklyn** class cruiser, but it was *the* **Brooklyn** herself. We all wanted to see our passage through this famous ditch, and were not disappointed. The Panama Canal is so brilliantly lighted at night that daylight was not missed.

Fuel was our worry. Would we make it to Cuba and Guantanamo Bay? Chief Machinist's Mate Spike was the 'oil king', the man who measured the 'bottoms' or 'voids' where we held our oil. It was he who decided which 'void' should be heated so the oil (like molasses at room temperature) could be moved to the burners. They had to be selected, first one side then the other, so the ship did not develop a list. He also was in charge of water consumption. We evaporated sea-water, using exhaust steam, condensed it into distilled water and used it for our own consumption as well as for replacing boiler water lost naturally in the operation of the turbines driving the ship (make-up feed). Quite a responsibility, but Chief Machinist's Mate Spike was good. We did make Guantanamo Bay, 'Gitmo' in Navy vernacular, but with only a few more days' oil left!

The tales of those who did go ashore in Cuba had to satisfy me. My headache of the last two days was too excruciating. When I finally gave up and saw Dr. Manlove, he suspected a lack of salt. I explained that, rather than take the huge salt pills (more suitable to a horse than a human) procured in New Zealand when we ran out of our own, I had been liberally dousing my meals with table salt. "Take these two salt pills right now, and fifteen minutes later take one more," he ordered. Miraculously, the headache was gone before the fifteen minutes was up. It was too late to arrange going ashore, so I skipped Cuba. I did not miss much, from what I was told. It would have been fun, however, to have witnessed the scene in the officers' club when one of the Naval Reserve aviators began throwing drinks, glass and all, at Mr. Herring, the ship's First Lieutenant. No Court-Martial for aviators, they are too valuable. Instead, this aviator was transferred to permanent shore-based flying.

Leaving Cuba, none of us knew where we were going. Only Captain Stone, and possibly Commander Denebrink, knew. Not even Mr. Cavenagh, my boss, knew. We did go north and entered the Gulf Stream. The ocean temperature abruptly rose many degrees at that time. We, in the engine room, reported the temperature readings to the bridge, which assisted the Navigator. It was before we had Radar, and every aid possible was used in navigation. Proceeding north, using the Gulf Stream to boost us, we finally saw Cape Cod. My first sight of our East Coast, just like my ancestors', was from the Atlantic. As we rounded Cape Cod into Cape Cod Bay, the scuttlebutt was finally firmed up. To Boston we were going.

As we tied up in the Boston Navy Yard, to our surprise and happiness we were greeted by all the ship's families from Hawaii! Talk about 'scuttlebutt'! When we didn't even know ourselves where we were going, how on earth did they know? It was reminiscent of the days of slavery when "[the slaves]…kept themselves informed of events by what was termed the 'grape-vine telegraph'."[38] The slaves knew the news before their masters.

To go back a few chapters to the 'bull Ensign', Arnold Jaeckel, – Jake and his wife were now living in Boston due to his graduate school classes at MIT. We were glad to see him again. They too knew we were coming, for the other officers' wives told them.

---

[38] Booker T. Washington, *Up From Slavery*, Chapter 1.

28
Blowing Tubes

Even a routine ship's procedure can result in an embarrassing event. Such was the case one sultry night while the **Brooklyn** was at sea in the tropics.

Any machinery powered by steam requires a boiler. Most boilers used for power are of two types, fire tube or water tube. Fire tube boilers have a multitude of tubes through which the flames travel, boiling the water in which the tubes are immersed. Water tube boilers, used in the **Brooklyn**, have water inside the tubes to be turned into steam by flames blazing around the outside of the tubes. Soot from the oil-fired flames gets deposited on the outside of these tubes, reducing their efficiency. To get rid of the soot, a rotating steam pipe with holes is built into each boiler; and, when it is turned on, jets of steam blow the soot off the tubes. This is known as 'blowing tubes'.[39]

The result of blowing tubes is a horrendous black cloud visible for many miles, even over the horizon, which is a dead giveaway to any enemy that other ships are in the area. It is therefore customary to blow tubes at night, usually an hour before dawn to give the cloud time to dissipate by

---

[39] Also known as 'blowing stacks', from which probably came the slang expression 'to blow one's stack.'

sunrise. The procedure aboard the **Brooklyn** (and probably the same in other ships) was for the Chief Water Tender in charge of the 'fire rooms' (boiler rooms) to call the engine room to ask permission to blow tubes. The Officer in Charge (OINC) of the engine room then would request permission from the bridge. Permission is not always given immediately. The engine room may be asked to wait until the ship has been turned so the wind is blowing across the ship. Otherwise the after part of the ship would receive a liberal deposit of black oily soot, wet with condensed steam, which could take great effort and time to clean. Ships of war turn frequently to confuse enemy submarines, so the engine room waits until the bridge gives permission after a 'zig' or a 'zag' has been made. Then the fire rooms are told it's now O.K. to blow tubes.

As we were steaming east along the equator, Captain Stone and Commander Denebrink decided that all senior officers should be able to run the ship from the bridge, *even the aviators*! One early morning, when I was OINC of the engine room, the Chief in charge of the fire rooms requested permission to blow tubes. I called the bridge to see if it was O.K.. The senior *aviator* had the conn and answered me breezily with "Sure, go ahead." So I went ahead. The senior aviator must have forgotten a few details of 'conning' (bossing) a ship since his graduation from the Naval Academy. **Brooklyn** should have been 'zagged.'

About this time, while the tubes were still being blown, I was relieved from watch and was making my way up the ladders ('stairs' to land-lubbers) to my cabin when I met the most miserable, wet, sooty, greasy sailors coming down the ladders from the deck. It was hot steaming along the equator, and many of the crew had been sleeping on deck. A heavy dew had just fallen and the soot joined in to make a horrible nightmare turn real to these unfortunates. I had to sidle my way up the ladders past them so as not to get any of that 'goop' on *my* uniform. These sailors were all 'blowing their stacks' at those 'so-and-sos' in the engine room. I felt that this was not the right time to explain our innocence to these poor souls, much less tell them I just came from the engine room.

In retrospect, I 'betcha' Stone and Denebrink figured *I* was the one responsible. They would never blame an Academy man, a Full Lieutenant at that, for the disaster, which, in a big way, was *their* fault.

The moral to this tale is: "Don't blow your stacks if you don't know the 'facks.'"

29
Heliotrope

When the crew last saw Heliotrope (named for her color), she was being pursued by seagulls in the Boston Navy Yard. Gulls do not think romantically about pigeons, we understand, so she was chased for some other reason. But, why was this Hawaiian bird in Boston in the first place?

Her story begins in spring, 1941, after Captain Stone took command of the **Brooklyn**. While we were at our mooring in Pearl Harbor, Captain Stone noticed a tame pigeon being fed by our cooks. She stayed with the ship, and Captain Stone took a liking to her, which was strange because he did not like human beings (we wondered if he liked to eat 'squab'). The ship's carpenters were ordered to build a nest for her on the after mast immediately above 'Sky Aft'.[40] Heliotrope moved into her new home and was content. The only flaw showed up during 'battle stations'. My cabin-mate Bob Woodall's battle station in Sky Aft was immediately under the nest. Poor Woodall: after his first time under the nest, he wore protective covering. You should have seen Woody's 'mess' uniform! The **Brooklyn**'s laundry had to scrape it before laundering.

---

[40] The anti-aircraft range-finder covering the sky behind the ship.

The aviators wondered about our pigeon's 'air speed'. At eighteen knots, our usual rate, Heliotrope might not make it back to the ship. Heliotrope was smart; she flew astern in the ship's back-draft. No lost pigeon from this ship! Only once was she in peril. When we were steaming along the equator, Heliotrope ventured too far to one side. Her epic struggle against the wind to make it back thrilled all. Never before has a pigeon 'winged it' so furiously. She finally gained our vacuum and safety.

Heliotrope became acquainted with Pago Pago[41] in Samoa along with us, and accompanied us on to New Zealand. None of those who saw it will ever forget Heliotrope's entry to Auckland harbor. We, in our best uniforms, and with stern determined faces, were lined up at 'Attention'. Salutes were fired ashore and afloat in the rites always performed while entering a major foreign port. All were impressed with the solemnity surrounding the arrival of United States Navy ships, the first since 1925. All, that is, except Heliotrope, who perched herself on the hat of a rigidly standing sailor and would not be shooed off. Laugh? It was hard not to! What did the New Zealanders think?

She kept with us from New Zealand to Tahiti, and thence back to Hawaii. Nothing of note happened to Heliotrope in Tahiti as far as we knew. Those Tahitian pigeons may have seduced Heliotrope when nobody was looking. The Papeete 'wahines' did quite a job seducing the crew.

In May, 1941, while on maneuvers, the 'beloved' Captain Stone received orders which changed the lives of all on board. We were going to the Atlantic! The details of my missed birthday 'luau' and our trip through Panama and on to Guantanamo Bay, Cuba, are in Chapter 27. Heliotrope stuck

---

[41] For Samoa stories, including fun events like the 'sword dance' performed on our deck, see Chapter 18.

with us through all this voyage until we tied up in Boston Navy Yard, where we stayed for a while.

We were docked next to the British battleship **H.M.S. Rodney**, just in from sinking the German battleship **Bismarck**. The **Rodney** people were upset. A late-comer, the *Admiral's* flagship **H.M.S. Dorsetshire**, having fired only *one* torpedo into the sinking **Bismarck,** was credited in all reports and in the news with the sinking! **Rodney**'s battle wounds were being repaired by our Navy Yard.

It was there, in the 'civilized' environs of the Boston Navy Yard, that Heliotrope attracted the attention of the seagulls, who chased her away. We believe the gulls wanted to eat Heliotrope's food (and probably eat Heliotrope, too). Seagulls are omnivorous; Heliotrope's food of grain and bread was just their ticket (and so was Heliotrope). Did she try to resist? We don't know, but we do know seagulls are notorious robbers and cannibals. We never saw Heliotrope again. A day of mourning was declared by Captain Stone, and all hands felt sorry (except Woodall).

30
Round Trip to Iceland

We left the Boston Navy Yard in late June, 1941, and put to sea. Off New York City we joined an 'armada'. There were three old battleships: **U.S.S. Arkansas, U.S.S. New York,** and **U.S.S. Texas**. There was another **Brooklyn** class cruiser: **U.S.S. Nashville** (CL-43). There were twenty-five destroyers, a supply ship, a tanker, and a sea-going tug. This collection of ships formed a 'Task Force' whose 'Task' was to protect five transports loaded with Marines – the reason for this armada. The battleships and cruisers were there in case any German battleships sortied out against us. Though the **Bismarck** had been sunk, Germany still had others. The twenty-five destroyers, with their Sonar equipment and depth charges, were to protect the transports from German U-boats. The tanker and supply ship were to replenish the Force at our rendezvous, which turned out to be Iceland. The sea-going tug? It was to tow any ship in the Force should it be disabled.

When hostilities began between England and Germany, England placed an Army of Occupation in Iceland. This move effectively blocked Germany from doing the same thing. The U.S. Marines in these five transports were to replace the British force, which was to return to England to fight the 'Battle of Britain'.

The first stop *en route* to Iceland was Argentia Bay, Newfoundland, where the personnel in the U.S. Navy enclave, seeing a mighty force coming up over the horizon, thought a German invasion force was about to land. Later that summer, in August, Roosevelt and Churchill met aboard **U.S.S. Augusta** (see p24 note 13) for a secret conference, later called the 'Atlantic' conference. When asked where the conference had taken place, Roosevelt answered, "Shangri-La." But I knew where Shangri-La was located. In the newspaper pictures, I recognized a strangely shaped island in the background. It was where we had anchored in Argentia Bay. An aircraft carrier was later named **U.S.S. Shangri-La** in honor of this important conference.

From Newfoundland the Task Force proceeded to Iceland, sinking two German submarines of the 'wolf pack', and a probable third , as related in Chapter 1. The explosions of the distant depth charges could be felt from my 'battle station' in the after engine room, but I had no idea what was going on during the battle. We 'got the word' when we were released from our 'battle stations' in the **Brooklyn**. We heard the destroyers have just sunk a German U-boat! How can this be? We are not at war with Germany in July of 1941. My first thought is that sinking ships of another country is 'piracy' if we are not at war.

The explanation for our sinking the U-boats, after it sifts down to us Ensigns, is, "Following orders." To 'time-travel' a bit, this was the defense used at the Nuremberg trials by the Nazis when WW II was over. I must admit our orders are valid. Our 'task' is to get the Marines safely from Newfoundland to Iceland. There is too much at stake to risk a submarine attack on these transports, even from a country at 'peace' with us. It is fitting that these unusual fireworks occurred on the Fourth of July. In my mind, even though we are not officially at war with Germany, we are in the fight. I am satisfied. This is why I am here as an officer in the United

States Navy (but I still think of the German U-boat crews going to their deaths).

Sinking of German U-boats continued after our 'Task' was completed. More Marines were sent to Iceland and had to be protected. There were perilous consequences. Destroyer **Reuben James** was sunk with much loss of life, and destroyer **Kearney** was towed to Qvalsjold Fjordur[42] (see next page) Iceland, in a half-sinking condition.

No protest was made to Germany by the United States for these actions. I think this was for complex reasons. Isolationist sentiment in the United States was almost universal, and any retaliation, even for the deaths of our sailors, was impossible. If a protest had been made, Germany could truthfully answer that the U-boats were acting in self-defense! That, in turn, would have revealed the many U-boat sinkings, outraging the isolationists, and impairing this undeclared war. It took a massive strike on December 7th to silence the isolationists and bring the country into 'real' war.

After the attack on Pearl Harbor on December 7th that year, those who were in service before that date were entitled to wear the 'American Defense Ribbon'. Those who were at sea during this time wore a star in the center of this decoration. A new honor was given: those who were in certain ships in certain time periods were entitled to wear an **A** in lieu of the star. The **A** denoted Action in the Atlantic prior to "the Day of Infamy." **Brooklyn** was one of the designated ships and I wore the **A** proudly. Later, when I reported for special detached duty in California, the commanding officer, a Lieutenant, asked me about the **A**. When I told him, he wouldn't believe me. I did not care. He could check with my unit in Washington if he pleased, but he let it go. Some people are officious!

---

[42] We had been anchored in this fjord in July, and I recognized it, though the papers did not tell the location.

One would think that seeing all the death about us as we crossed the Grand Banks following a tragic convoy would be enough. Not for Captain Stone, who shot a porpoise from the bridge. Two porpoises were playfully swimming alongside the ship, and Stone left one dying in its own blood. Captain Stone was far removed from Captain Smith in personality! I saw this act, for I had to be on the bridge to direct de-gaussing settings as we crossed the shallow water of the Banks. I wished I hadn't. My feelings may have showed.

We made it safely to Iceland and unloaded the transports in Reykjavik. Next to Reykjavik was a fjord going inland a few miles, called Qvalsjold Fjordur (Whale Fjord), ending in a large circular basin. Already at anchor there was a British battleship, but there was still room for all the Task Force except the transports – the whole works fit in there easily. We were there for fifteen days. It was hard to know when to hit the sack, because it was light all night in midsummer.

There were rumors that a German air raid was imminent, but Hitler didn't risk it. He wasn't ready for the United States as an enemy.

Once our hiking bunch thought it would be fun to hike on a pretty green meadow we could see from our ship; so we had one of the ship's boats take us there and drop us off. We were surprised when we got to the edge of this 'meadow' to discover that it was no meadow at all, but rather a swamp with three inches of water all the way across! We had to cross it, though, because we had told the crew of the ship's boat to pick us up later on the other side. I wished we could have turned back, because we all ended up with soggy shoes and sopping wet socks.

I went into Reykjavik for a day's leave. A destroyer was used to transport us to and from the city – the first and last time I'd ever been aboard a destroyer. Robert Ripley said that the most beautiful women in the world live in Iceland,

'Believe It Or Not'. After seeing the women in Reykjavik, I go along with Ripley.

In Reykjavik, I bought some souvenirs, including an enormous wheel of bleu cheese for my delightful cousin, Bette Cooper,[43] who enjoyed good things to eat. It was about eight inches in diameter and four inches high, and I was going to mail it to her home in Hackettstown, New Jersey, upon our return to the States. Alas, I hadn't reckoned with my rapacious Annapolis comrades. A large wheel of bleu cheese is impossible to hide, and it was sitting on my desk in my cabin, right out in the open. They would come in armed with table knives and big boxes of crackers they had gotten from the galley. What was I going to do to protect my cheese – stab them with my sword? That wheel of cheese lasted only three days. I did visit Bette Cooper on my return – not empty-handed, because luckily I had also bought her a pair of beautiful sealskin mittens. But for the rest, she had to be contented with the story of The Cheese That Got Away.

After fifteen days in Iceland, we departed and traveled directly to Norfolk Navy Yard. Now that my one-year probation period was ending, I was expecting to be detached from the **Brooklyn**. I wasn't sorry to be leaving this once-happy ship.

---

[43] Miss America, 1937.

31
Goodbye, U.S.S. Brooklyn

When my one year afloat probation period was over, Executive Officer Commander F.C. Denebrink was only too happy to detach me from the **Brooklyn** in Norfolk to await further orders. This would-be 'Queeg',[44] whose sadistic urges had been held in check by Captain Smith, found them unleashed when like-minded Captain Stone took over. As an example, the two-man 'brig' – hitherto unused – within one month had a two-month waiting list of Prisoners at Large (PAL) – restricted to the ship until their jail sentences had been served. What had been a happy ship was now sad.

Commander Denebrink early showed his scorn of my status as a Navy officer. I was not only a Reserve officer (the only one aboard at first except for the aviators) and not an Academy graduate, but I was also designated for Engineering duty only. In his mind, there was nothing lower than either category, and I combined both. His animosity contrasted with the other 'trade school' (Annapolis) graduates who treated me with the same friendship and camaraderie (like eating my pineapples and cheese) as their fellows. I did not endear myself to Denebrink on one occasion in his office. He was extolling the rigors of an Academy education. "Of all the Midshipmen appointed to the Academy, 15% don't make it."

---

[44] *The Caine Mutiny*. Herman Wouk, 1951.

"That is a coincidence, Commander. Of all the Freshmen who entered Purdue with me, 15% *did* make it." The 'ninety-day wonders' who later reported to the ship were acceptable to Denebrink, for they were *deck* Officers!

With three others detached from the ship at the same time[45], I moved to a rooming house in Virginia Beach, where one of us phoned Norfolk Navy Yard every morning to see if any of our orders had come in. After a month of 'paid vacation,' my orders came. I was to report to the Naval Reserve Armory in Chicago to be detached while awaiting my permanent commission.

On the way to Chicago, I decided to call at the Navy Bureau of Engineering in Washington. I had the feeling that Denebrink might have sabotaged my future in the Navy, perhaps to the extreme of denying my permanent commission, but the Bureau people welcomed me with obvious pleasure. I was the 'pat solution' to a difficult request from the Bureau of Personnel for an Ensign from the Fleet with engineering qualifications (preferably electrical) for temporary duty in Chicago (!) followed again by sea duty. The request was so unusually narrow they were wondering just where to find this rare officer – would they have to pull someone from sea duty? – when I 'fell into their laps from the sea'. I was told to continue as before and get my permanent commission, and they would send orders to await me at the Armory in Chicago. I could not learn what my new orders were. They would not talk. Most mysterious!

---

[45] Chief Machinist's Mate Spike (the 'oil king') had been promoted to Warrant Officer, and it was not 'policy' to retain an officer in the ship where he had been an enlisted man. Ensign Wakefield succumbed to sea-sickness in rough weather. Ensign Brekke was probably with us because his name began with a B instead of a W. (The names of all the other V-12 Ensigns on board started with W.)

32
Cipher Machine School

"Can you type?" asked Wilmer Worthy Weber, Executive Officer to the Commanding Officer of the U.S. Naval Inspector's office in the Board of Trade Building in Chicago. "No, Commander," I replied. "You will," he said, chuckling. The Captain (whose name I forget, but who could forget a name like the Commander's?) also laughed. I had no idea what they were talking about, and I still type by the 'hunt and peck' system. Giving me directions to the *Teletype Corporation*, they told me to report to the civilian Naval Inspector there, one Oliver Brown.[46] I was to assist him in his inspecting. I guessed I could inspect 'Navals' as well as anyone!

Oliver ('Pappy') Brown introduced me to five other Ensigns who were at *Teletype* for the same reason. It was then that I realized why my orders were so 'hush-hush' – *Teletype* was manufacturing vital cipher machines for both the U.S. Navy and the U.S. Army. It was the job of the six of us not just to assist 'Pappy' Brown, but also to become so

---

[46] Oliver Brown, a native of Oklahoma, was first cousin to a beautiful and popular singer, Grace Moore, who was killed in a plane crash in a river in Spain during World War II. Actor Leslie Howard perished also.

familiar with the machines that we could maintain them in good repair at sea or ashore. The reason for the strange request by the Bureau of Personnel became clear to me. None of the other five, all '90-Day Wonders,' had ever had any active duty experience at all, much less being at sea. They were all engineers, however. It was thought that by assigning me to the job, I would add 'salt' to the mixture as well as stabilize the group[47]. I believe I did that.

Our inspecting the machines took a load off of 'Pappy' Brown. It was our job to inspect all connections to insure enough heat had been applied to make good solder joints. Faulty 'cold-soldered' joints where the wire just fell off had been discovered in the field; we were to prevent future disasters with our inspection. We also typed messages to be deciphered by us on other machines. "The quick brown fox jumped over the lazy dogs back" came out on the other machine with 'laxy dog' because 'space' was enciphered as a 'z', and 'z' was enciphered as 'x'. It was figured there would be no mistake in the meaning with this arrangement. Some of our messages were (ahem!) not 'nice' when deciphered.

The school involved complete assembly and dis-assembly of a machine. In addition to this, our instructor, Carl A. Levin, the engineer who had put the machine into production at *Teletype*, threw the problems at us which had happened at *Teletype* during manufacture. Things like unhooking a spring or dirtying a contact gave all sorts of weird symptoms which we were soon adept at finding and rectifying.

For our 'final exam' problem, Cal Levin gave us a 'humdinger' which had baffled *Teletype* engineers for weeks. Some of the machines were equipped to run in 'tandem'. Hooked together by a massive cable plugged into the back of

---

[17] Those names I can remember are: George Dorsey, Dermot Edmundson (100% Irish ancestry), and Ensigns Shelley and Williams. The other name escapes me.

each machine, one machine deciphered into plain text what was being enciphered by the other. This automatically checked the machines in the field to prevent errors. The two machines Cal fixed up for us each worked fine individually, but when connected, chaos resulted.

The other five 'students' tried all the things they had learned, and were getting nowhere. I took the wiring diagram to one side and pored over it. When I told Cal I had the solution, he took me to one side so as not to 'spoil' it for the others. In the wiring of the rear receptacles were two yellow wires adjacent to each other; one was a 'fat' one for power, while the other was a 'skinny' message wire. I figured if the two were transposed, a 'mish-mash' would happen, but only when the machines were cabled together, and it did. Visual inspection showed two yellow wires connected where they were supposed to be, and the size difference would be a subtle thing, not readily noticed during inspection. It took me about thirty minutes to solve this, without even touching the machines, but it changed the course of my life.

33
December 7th 1941!

It was a day like any Sunday since my return from the year at sea. In civilian attire, as all officers wore in peacetime when not aboard a ship or Naval base, I went to the movies with my high-school friend, Norris Coambs and his wife, Harriet. On the way home we stopped for refreshments at a drugstore soda fountain (practically non-existent these days). To my unbelieving dismay, I heard people talking about "Pearl Harbor being bombed." When I got home, my mother told me a man had called to say I was to wear my uniform on Monday. Listening to the radio that night, I heard awful stories of what had happened that morning. Ships with which I was familiar were on the bottom! How hard it was to believe what I was hearing. My mother was not as surprised as I was. For years, she had been a member of an organization called Stop Arming Japan, which endeavored to stop shipments of scrap steel to Japan, saying they would be returned to us in death! Sometimes the group was successful. Sagacious Mother!

The next morning, I boarded my usual elevated train and was the focus of astonished stares from passengers whose faces had become familiar through the last few months. Did they, in inland Chicago, recognize a Navy officer's uniform? Little do we realize, sometimes, who rides next to us as we go on our daily routine.

Arriving at *Teletype*, I hadn't been at the job more than an hour or so when I was called into the *Teletype* President's office. There I was informed that one of the six of us officers was to go to fortress Corregidor in Manila Bay, the Philippines, to keep the cipher machines running. I was the one selected; based mainly on the very strong recommendation of our instructor, 'Cal' Levin, seconded by Naval Inspector 'Pappy' Brown, and further endorsed by the Inspector's office. I was told I was to return to the Inspector's office in the Board of Trade building for additional instruction. At that office, I was told to go home and pack up for imminent departure.

That Monday night, I went to Alex Hussey's house, where we listened to news of Hawaii on his short-wave radio. A day or two later, Alex called me with very bad family news. The day after the attack, Sam Hussey and his neighbors were building a bomb shelter under his house. A concrete block fell on Sam's foot and he was taken to the hospital. Because of Sam's prominence, he was given an injection of the new and rare drug, penicillin. In a short while Sam was dead! He was not killed by the Japanese; he was killed by World War I. Trench warfare had left Sam with severe asthma. The mold, *Penicillium*, from which penicillin is derived, together with the lasting effect of the mold from the trenches, produced too much of an anaphylactic shock (allergic reaction) for my good friend Sam to withstand. Progress continues for the benefit of mankind, but the benefits are not always universal.

Because of the post-attack turmoil, the Navy didn't issue my orders until January 4th, 1942. They stated, "Proceed to the Washington Navy Yard, report to the Naval Code and Signal Laboratory, and there wait for first available government transportation (FAGTRANS) to Manila,

Philippine Islands, and from there proceed to Cavite Navy Yard and report to the Officer in Charge for further duty."

While waiting for orders, I dated Dorothy Shawhan. Dorothy was introduced to me at a party celebrating my return from sea, by my Purdue classmate Glen Bigelow and his wife, Kay. Knowing I would probably not return from the Philippines, for cryptographic people would not fare well in the hands of the Japanese, I knew better than to be serious with her, though I liked her a lot. She was woefully ignorant of the Navy and thought I would be dressed in a 'sailor suit' for our first meeting. For that pre-Pearl Harbor dating, I wore civilian clothes. After Pearl Harbor, the civilian clothes were put aside for years. Now to get to the Philippines via Washington.

Figure 8, Downtown Chicago - With Dorothy
Shawhan, later to be Mrs Cragg, between
December 7, 1941 and January 4, 1942. Waiting
for orders to the Philippines via Washington, DC.

Figure 9, Dating Dorothy Shawhan. December, 1941

Epilogue

After I left the **Brooklyn**, it went on to serve in many other important missions, such as shelling the French fleet in Morocco in 1942. It was involved in the rescue of the crew of the burning Coast Guard ship **U.S.C.G.S. Wakefield**, and in the bombardment of the French fleet in Casablanca harbor while protecting transports waiting to unload troops. It roved the west coast of Italy with the 'Galloping Ghost of the Italian coast', **U.S.S. Philadelphia**. Off the coast of Italy, she struck a mine – casualties: one broken leg and a short term in dry-dock. Several years after the War was over, **Brooklyn** was sold to Chile, where she was renamed The **Generalissimo Bernardo O'Higgins**. In spite of the rescue efforts by the *U.S.S. Brooklyn Association*, she has been sold for scrap metal. I attend the **Brooklyn**'s yearly reunions whenever I can, now that Denebrink is gone.

I never got to Manila, luckily for me, since the Japanese had invaded the Philippines by the time I arrived in Washington, D.C. "Who would you report to, Tojo?" asked Commander Groseclose, commander of the Radio Laboratory which contained the Naval Code and Signal Laboratory. I was assigned to the NCSL eventually, and it was there that I did what I consider my most important work during the War, though much of it has had to remain secret all these years.

Volume II of these memoirs will include my solution to a German U-boat *Enigma* cipher machine problem, and other activities while I was officer in charge of Research and Development at the Naval Code and Signal Laboratory. This sequel will also describe my travels concerning cipher machines located in such far-flung outposts as Dutch Harbor, Alaska, and Halifax, Nova Scotia, as well as my training of a crew of WAVES, most of whom thought they were going to be secretaries to Admirals, to solder wires onto lugs in cipher machine components. They might have thought this was a come-down, but it was an extremely important task, key to the war effort.

As for Dorothy Shawhan, whom I had been casually dating in the previous chapter, ...I married her!

Appendix 1
A Primer for Landlubbers

I have been told that many of the terms and expressions I take for granted need some explanation for those unfamiliar with ships and the Navy, so here is some additional information for landlubbers. This is not intended to be a handbook for new recruits, however! For more information, see for example:
http://www.history.navy.mil/index.html.

More U.S. Navy vessel information is in a ***German*** (!) website: http://www.skyrocket.de/usnavy/

Ratings and Ranks as they were during World War II. Most have since changed.

On the next page is a partial list of ratings (enlisted men) and ranks (officers), starting at the top and going all the way down to where I began, as Fireman 3rd Class.

Flag Officers[48]
>   Admiral of the Fleet (5 stars)
>   Admiral (4 stars)
>   Vice Admiral (3 stars)
>   Rear Admiral (2 stars)
>   Commodore (1 star)

Other Commissioned Officers
>   Captain
>   Commander
>   Lieutenant Commander
>   Lieutenant
>   Lieutenant (jg)
>   Ensign

Warrant Officers
>   Chief Warrant Officer
>   Warrant Officer

Petty Officers (Mates[49])
>   Chief Petty Officer
>   Petty Officer 1st Class
>   Petty Officer 2nd Class
>   Petty Officer 3rd Class

Lower Ratings
>   Seaman/Fireman 1st Class
>   Seaman/Fireman 2nd Class
>   Fireman 3rd Class

---

[48]So-called because a special flag is flown to show that an Admiral is on board a ship or station.

[49]The different divisions call these petty officers 'mates', for example, *Machinist's Mate 1st Class* in the Engineering Divisions.

Appendix 2
Salmon O. Levinson

Murder! Murder and kidnaping most foul! A bloody deed was committed in 1924 by young Leopold and Loeb in my neighborhood, and I could have been the victim!

Living next door to millionaire lawyer Salmon O. Levinson on Chicago's South Side became perilous in 1924, when it was revealed by the confession of Nathan Leopold that the kidnap-murderers Leopold and Loeb had parked in front of *my* house many times while lying in wait for son Johnny Levinson, a cousin of Loeb's and their primary target, to come home from 'The Harvard School for Boys.' Johnny never came home when expected because he was in one of the many after-school play 'gangs' coached by some University of Chicago 'Phys. Ed.' majors. Leopold and Loeb finally gave up on Johnny Levinson and sought other prey. The killers happened upon another cousin of Loeb's, Bobby Franks, who willingly accepted a 'lift' from his cousin, Dick Loeb. Once in the car, Bobby was bludgeoned to death by Leopold from the back seat. This pair of teen-aged villains secreted the body south of Chicago in swampland hauntingly described by Midwest poet Carl Sandburg in *Prairie Waters by Night*: "...Chatter of birds raises a night song [Leopold was an avian expert who knew the area well]...and the long willows drowse...and sleep on the shoulders of the running water."[50] Such was the requiem for poor Bobby Franks.

Another potential victim of this pair was yet another cousin of Loeb's, my good friend from second grade (after he was transferred from *The Harvard School For Boys* [!] because of the killing), Dick Schwartz. Dick told me a lurid detail of the murder not revealed in the newspapers. (In the 1920s, even the 'yellow press' of William Randolph Hearst would not print the shockingly lewd and gory items common in today's 'check-out line' magazines.) Dick told me that after being beaten to death, Bobby Franks was mutilated to make it appear he was a girl. Leopold and Loeb reasoned – with their phenomenal I-Q s of 185 and 210 – that if Bobby's body was discovered, identification would be impossible. It didn't work. They were super-intelligent, but had no 'street smarts.' All this was too close to me for comfort. My parents were shocked! However, I was safe, I think. My father was not a millionaire, and I was no relation to Richard Loeb. I would not go for a ride with strangers.

Neighbor Levinson determined, when I was but eleven, the size of the ship I was to live in for a year when I was twenty-three. Levinson was awarded the Nobel Peace Prize for his authorship of the 'Kellogg Peace Pact' signed in 1928 by fifteen nations. The pact included an arms limitation treaty between the three major naval powers. In this treaty, new warship construction was agreed to be in the proportion – by weight – of 5-5-3 (United States, Great Britain, and Japan respectively.) My ship of the future, **U.S.S. Brooklyn**, to be commissioned in 1937, would be one of the 10,000 ton cruisers (13,000 tons when fully loaded) whose maximum weight was limited by the treaty. To compensate for this limitation, **Brooklyn** would be crammed with devastating fire-power in the form of fifteen 6-inch guns, plus auxiliary armament of eight multi-purpose (anti-aircraft and surface) 5-

---

[50] *Poetry Magazine*, Chicago, 1916.

inch guns, besides heavy machine guns and other small arms! The **Brooklyn**, in mid-1941[51], would be berthed for a short time in the Boston Navy Yard next to British battleship **H.M.S. Rodney**, sinker of the **Bismarck**, and a casualty of the Kellogg Peace Pact. Partially completed when the Pact was signed, **Rodney** had three of its 14-inch guns deleted when its stern was 'bob-tailed' to meet the weight restrictions. The Boston Navy Yard was to repair battle damage from the **Bismarck** encounter.

---

[51]as described in Chapter 29 *Heliotrope.*

Appendix 3
Head Rails and Poop Decks

Sailing warships had three 'head rails' on each side at the bow (or head) of the ship. While appearing ornamental, these rails served as the toilet for the enlisted men. Staggered outward from the bottom, the lower rail was called the 'foot rail' for that was where a sailor placed his feet. The top rail was known as the 'hair rail' because a sailor leaned back against it, being careful not to get his pigtail caught in a splinter. The middle rail, where the sailor sat, was known as the [word deleted] rail.

When a sailor said he was going to the head, that was literally what he meant. In these days of modern conveniences, and when toilets can now be placed anywhere in the ship, they are still called 'heads.' (Navy nomenclature is conservative.) As for the officers, they went aft where there were no splashing bow waves, using, of course, the 'poop rail' which fenced the 'poop deck' at the stern.

(From a letter written by Rear Admiral John W. Schmidt, USN Ret. - Artist - my advisor for the **Erie** painting)

Figure 10, U.S. Ship-Sloop **Erie**. Painting by author.

Figure 11, The Head.

Finis

Made in the USA
Monee, IL
07 July 2026

56551284R00083